MW00653405

Christ's Body, Christ's Wounds

Christ's Body, Christ's Wounds

*Staying Catholic When You've
Been Hurt in the Church*

EDITED BY
Eve Tushnet

FOREWORD BY
Elizabeth Scalia

CASCADE *Books* · Eugene, Oregon

CHRIST'S BODY, CHRIST'S WOUNDS
Staying Catholic When You've Been Hurt in the Church

Copyright © 2018 Wipf and Stock Publishers. All rights reserved. Except for brief quotations in critical publications or reviews, no part of this book may be reproduced in any manner without prior written permission from the publisher. Write: Permissions, Wipf and Stock Publishers, 199 W. 8th Ave., Suite 3, Eugene, OR 97401.

Cascade Books
An Imprint of Wipf and Stock Publishers
199 W. 8th Ave., Suite 3
Eugene, OR 97401

www.wipfandstock.com

PAPERBACK ISBN: 978-1-5326-1373-9
HARDCOVER ISBN: 978-1-5326-1375-3
EBOOK ISBN: 978-1-5326-1374-6

Cataloguing-in-Publication data:

Names: Tushnet, Eve, editor. | Scalia, Elizabeth, foreword.

Title: Christ's body, Christ's wounds : staying Catholic when you've been hurt in the church / edited by Eve Tushnet ; foreword by Elizabeth Scalia.

Description: Eugene, OR : Cascade Books, 2018 | Includes bibliographical references.

Identifiers: ISBN 978-1-5326-1373-9 (paperback) | ISBN 978-1-5326-1375-3 (hardcover) | ISBN 978-1-5326-1374-6 (ebook)

Subjects: LCSH: Catholic Church—Apologetic works. | Catholic Church—Membership.

Classification: BX1752 .C44 2018 (print) | BX1752 .C44 (ebook)

Scripture texts in this work are taken from the *New American Bible, revised edition* © 2010, 1991, 1986, 1970 Confraternity of Christian Doctrine, Washington, D.C. and are used by permission of the copyright owner. All Rights Reserved. No part of the New American Bible may be reproduced in any form without permission in writing from the copyright owner.

Manufactured in the U.S.A.   01/25/18

*For those who seek witnesses and
companions on the journey*

Contents

CONTENTS

Part III: Reclaiming the Faith

Contributors

Catherine Addington is a writer from Alexandria, Virginia.

Gabriel Blanchard is a California native living in Baltimore, a Catholic convert and a nap enthusiast. He has published a novel (*Death's Dream Kingdom*) and a collection of poems (*Wells of Night*), and blogs at *Mudblood Catholic* on theology, sexuality, art, and politics—and is not hiding inside the crawlspace of your house.

Joanne Butler is a cradle Catholic and was a National Latin Scholar in high school. An economist, she is a graduate of the Kennedy School of Government at Harvard and resides on the East Coast.

"Casey" is a freelance writer, documentary filmmaker, and new mom. Not necessarily in that order.

M. Saverio Clemente is a husband and father of two. He lives in Massachusetts where he writes, studies, and teaches philosophy.

Dana Sprott Cunningham is a fifth-generation Catholic of African-American descent who has been actively involved in many parishes. She is married to Thomas, with children Thomas, Fr. Curtis MC, and Toni, and three grandchildren.

Zach Czaia is a poet, editor, and teacher. His first book of poems, *Saint Paul Lives Here (In Minnesota)*, was published by Wipf and Stock in 2015.

"**Elena**" is a Dallas native. She earned an art degree at a Catholic university and has five children.

Jason E. Gillikin cofounded Caffeinated Press, a small independent book-publishing company focused on West Michigan talent. He earned a BA in moral philosophy and political science and currently resides in Grand Rapids, Michigan, with two cats, a passel of friends, and a battle-tested relationship with the Lord.

Rachel LaPointe is a cradle Catholic from Michigan, mom of four amazing children, and married to the best husband ever. She loves social media, books, lively debates, and a good bottle of stout.

Paula Gonzales Rohrbacher is a Catholic activist, wife, mother, blogger, and cofounder of RUaH, a compassionate listening ministry for those who have been harmed by representatives of the Catholic Church. She lives in Douglas, Alaska, with her husband, Charles, and her two dogs: Frida, a diabolical Dachshund, and Beans, a saintly Westie.

"**Sarah**" is an occasional freelance writer and artist who is grateful for the gifts of Catholicism, the Deaf community, and American Sign Language.

Elizabeth Scalia is Editor-in-Chief at Aleteia.org (English) and the author of *Strange Gods: Unmasking the Idols in Everyday Life*.

Eve Tushnet is the author of *Gay and Catholic: Accepting My Sexuality, Finding Community, Living My Faith* (Ave Maria 2014) and *Amends: A Novel* (CreateSpace 2015). She lives in Washington, DC.

Foreword

ELIZABETH SCALIA

H ow can you love what has hurt you? How can you go back?

I don't know.

A long time ago I shared a story from my life with someone: a story of repeated sexual abuse by a family member I had loved, and hated. Someone whose death broke my heart, but whom I, for years, fantasized killing. With a shotgun, cleverly hidden in a box of long-stemmed roses.

My friend wondered how I could ever have forgiven him— how I could reconcile anything after such betrayal and pain. "It's complicated," I said. He hurt me profoundly, in ways that will affect me forever, and yet he also was the only person I can re- member ever reading me a bedtime story. He dishonored me and disrespected me in the physical—and quite frankly tortured my spirit and psyche—but he also honored my intellect, engaging me in challenging, intriguing discussions on politics and literature and sports, when no one else had a word to say to me beyond, "Do the dishes!"

When I was little and sick, he was the only one to bring me a stuffed toy.

When someone has given you the message, since infancy, that you are loved, and special enough to be read to—loved enough to die for, if it came to that—and then warps and distorts that mes- sage even as the relationship continues, yes, it's complicated. The only way to transcend the confusion is to believe a few things, with your whole heart:

1. That the apology you have sought, when finally offered, is sincere.

2. That the act of forgiveness doesn't change what is true, but it is essential to your own healing.

3. That you need the specific healing that comes with forgiving because you have been much sinned against, and very likely have sinned against someone else—differently, but still hurtfully, and so mercy matters.

4. That some part of the love you learned early on was completely, inarguably true, and because it was true, it has a light you can return to, must return to, in order to go on.

The essays shared in this slim volume illustrate a startlingly similar dynamic. What makes the familial abuse situation so deeply complex exists also between the Catholic Church and those who have been treated with a shattering cruelty by her clergy or her esteemed members. The Church, through her leaders and liturgies, delivered to us the great stories, all of them threaded with a theme of unending love. It consoled us when we were sick, fed us with the bread of life, and honored our intellects with challenging and well-reasoned teaching. And too often it abused and confused.

Sexual or psychological abuse is always evil, always damaging, but when it comes mixed with the messages of abiding love, from the (ostensibly) most trustworthy sector of one's life, well. . . how can you love what has hurt you? How can you go back?

I don't know. But I can attest that there is power in the going back. There is power in the act of working out one's healing, and there is power in the truth. In fact, once the truth has been spoken aloud and heard, the only place it can go, then, is to the source of all that is completely, inarguably, eternally, True.

Power to power; light to light; love to love. It all begets and assists grace.

Acknowledgments

B Y FAR THE BIGGEST debt I owe is to the contributors who so generously and often courageously shared their stories. I also thank those who considered contributing and spoke or wrote to me personally about their experiences, even though for many reasons they decided they weren't yet ready to discuss those experiences publicly. I'm grateful to everyone described in these works who has helped the contributors see the Church as a place of love and healing, not simply betrayal and pain.

And I'm very grateful to my copyeditor at Wipf and Stock, Brian Palmer, and everyone who worked with me there to bring this book into print. A book of this kind isn't an obvious crowd-pleaser, but they saw how much it was needed.

Finally, let me thank Ivan Plis for the poignant and spiritually rich image in the book's title. We do not know the body of Christ if we cannot see its wounds.

Introduction:
Songs of Perseverance

Eve Tushnet

> [T]he only thing that makes the Church endurable is that
> it is somehow the body of Christ and that on this we are
> fed. It seems to be a fact that you have to suffer as much
> from the Church as for it but if you believe in the divinity
> of Christ, you have to cherish the world at the same time
> that you struggle to endure it.
>
> —Flannery O'Connor, *The Habit of Being*[1]

CATHOLICS LOVE CONVERSION STORIES, for the same reason everybody loves rom-coms. We get to watch somebody fall in love with the faith, overcome obstacles, and at last reach the altar—and then we fade to black. The story stops right when it gets interesting; right when the hard part starts.

The radio program *This American Life* made the point in their 2009 episode "Somewhere Out There." Ira Glass interviews an American man who went on a ridiculously romantic quest for a Chinese opera musician—a woman he'd fallen for, though he didn't even know her name.

But the interview isn't really about that. It's about the rest of the story: They did marry, but as Glass explains, "it was really hard. The novelty had worn off and the framework of their entire

---

1. Flannery O'Connor, *The Habit of Being: Letters of Flannery O'Connor*, ed. Sally Fitzgerald (New York: Farrar, Straus, and Giroux, 1979) 90.

relationship was an ocean away . . . After going through those rough years when they even considered splitting up, the story of how they met came to feel less and less important and they didn't talk about it as much. Now they have a different story." The husband, Eric Hayot, describes it as "the story of struggle and pain passed through, and fought through, and overcome. And that's a story that you don't tell in public because no one ever asks how did you two stay together? Everyone always asks how did you two meet?"[2]

This anthology asks how people stay. What does it look like to stay Catholic, when you have been seriously harmed by other Catholics? What does it look like to remain within the Church, or to return, when your trust has been betrayed? Why—and *how*—do people stick it out through the hardest parts?

I started thinking about this book because I kept meeting these people. My own writing focuses on gay Catholics. I've led a charmed life in the Church, and have experienced relatively little of the suspicion and bigotry many other gay Christians have experienced from our fellow churchgoers. But if you write a book called *Gay and Catholic*[3] it turns out that lots of people will come up to you and tell you their stories.

Many of these stories were about growing up gay in the Church. But if you get a reputation for talking about difficult subjects in Christian life, people will come to you to pour out their hearts about totally *different* difficult subjects. And so I began to realize how many stories of perseverance were going untold. So many people would tell me about their experiences with single motherhood, with infertility, with loneliness. Sometimes they'd tell me about finding resources within the Church to address their suffering. Other times they'd tell me about cruel comments from strangers, or callous advice from priests. I began to see that everybody in the pews has a story, which is often much more

2. "Somewhere Out There," *This American Life*, WBEZ, New York, NY, February 13, 2009.

3. Eve Tushnet, *Gay and Catholic: Accepting My Sexuality, Finding Community, Living My Faith*, (Notre Dame, IN: Ave Maria, 2014).

harrowing and beautiful and interesting than their conversion story: a story of staying.

This anthology is not intended as an argument. The authors are not saying, "Here's why you should stay in the Catholic Church, even if other Catholics have made you suffer and told you it was God's will." There are other books to give you that perspective if you are interested in it, whether you want high-octane theology or popular interpretations. This book isn't, "You *should*"; it's, "God is with you, and you *can*."

These are stories of resilience. They depict honestly a Church beset by all the evils of the outside world: racism, gossip, violence, lies, and more. But these stories also explore the resonant truths of the gospel. These are stories of God's mercy, of the long hard road toward forgiveness, of hope and of honest wrestling with doubt.

The authors have had widely varying experiences, and they write in very different styles. You'll find poetry here, memoir, meditations on the lives of the saints, practical advice, and moral theology.

But you'll also find some unexpected harmonies. Because these stories cover such divergent experiences, they offer surprising insights about the common ground we find in our faith. For example, both Dana Cunningham's family memoir of surviving racism and M. Saverio Clemente's Augustine-influenced essay on a cousin ostracized by the community touch on the need to turn *ourselves* over to God when we have been sinned against. Jesus' commands to forgive and humble ourselves do not apply only to our tormentors, but to us as well.

Many of the essays, such as Elena's description of discovering Jesus as a loving friend rather than an angry abuser, touch on the connection between healing our own wounds and learning the true nature of God's love. We are all made in the image of God. Only in learning to see God's true face—not the lies we were taught—can we learn the truth about our own experiences.

Many of these essays include depictions of the good that priests can do. A compassionate priest who speaks a word of mercy at the right time plays a key role in so many stories of staying

Catholic. Those who need to know what a *good* shepherd looks like—and those who want to be good shepherds to people in distress—can find many examples in these pages.

The collection includes survivors of sexual abuse and virulent racism. But people suffer and struggle in the Church for all kinds of reasons that don't make the headlines. So the collection also includes a mom whose parish couldn't put up with her big family, and a gay Catholic who is faithful to the Church yet gets treated like a political slogan instead of a child of God.

The stories all have some darkness in them. If conversion stories are our Easter, these stories are the Acts of the Apostles, full of conflict and even martyrdom. But each story also offers a ray of hope. Some are very practical. Joanne Butler, whose donations were embezzled by her priest, gives a forthright call for a lay finance council in every parish. Some of these authors found new communities within the Church, as in Sarah's discovery of the faith of Deaf Catholics. Others found that the picture of God and the Church which they had been taught was incomplete or warped; they renewed their faith by reshaping it, as in Catherine Addington's depiction of reclaiming her relationship with the saints.

Above all, each essay or poem is itself a witness: you can face the truth about the evil things Catholics do to one another, and still love God and practice your faith.

Part I: Good and Bad Shepherds

This first part explores the struggle to rebuild your faith when your trust has been betrayed by someone in authority—someone who claimed to speak for God.

Paula Gonzales Rohrbacher, who testified before the United States Conference of Catholic Bishops about her sexual abuse by a seminarian, explains what it was like to testify, and how she has navigated her faith while living in the whirlwind of the Catholic sex-abuse scandal. She describes the priests and bishops who supported her and the reactions in her hometown that shocked her.

Zach Czaia offers both new and previously published poems meditating on the abuse scandals in the Archdiocese of Saint Paul and Minneapolis. Czaia includes work from his collection *Saint Paul Lives Here (In Minnesota)* in this anthology, used by permission of Wipf and Stock Publishers, as well as a new poem.

Casey depicts her relationship with a man who claimed he could help her heal after a rape—a man who couldn't have been more Catholic, "a regular at Adoration," but also a man who manipulated her into sex and made her feel that God had turned away from her. She describes her gradual rediscovery of a God of mercy and love.

And **Elena** describes the way a compassionate priest—and the Byzantine Catholic liturgy—helped her heal not only from sexual abuse at a Catholic school, but from the warped images the school had given her of God. Hers is a gently written but powerful indictment of "purity" obsession in the Catholic world and a creative depiction of, as Elena puts it, "leaving the 'angry Jesus' behind."

From Fear to Compassion

PAULA GONZALES ROHRBACHER

I WAS BORN INTO A Catholic family in Portland, Oregon. I attended parochial school for twelve years, and after graduating from high school, continued to attend Mass, because it never occurred to me to do otherwise. I joined the Jesuit Volunteer Corps after college and served for two years in Juneau, Alaska, where I eventually made my home. I joined our parish and became a music minister and an Extraordinary Minister of Holy Communion. My husband Charles and I were married at our parish, the Cathedral of the Nativity of the Blessed Virgin Mary. My children attended primary and high school religious education, and in August of this year, Charles will be celebrating his tenth anniversary of his ordination as a Permanent Deacon.

When I was eleven, I was molested by a seminarian, a so-called friend of our family, who was on break from school and staying at our house that summer. I didn't disclose at the time of the abuse because I was afraid of the effect it would have on my family, especially my mother. I kept the secret until I was twenty-nine years old and pregnant with my first child. My mother had come up to Alaska to visit me and brought José, the man who abused me. The news of their upcoming visit sent me into an emotional breakdown and I told Charles what had happened to me as a child. I began therapy and the long process of healing. Eventually, I told my mother and the rest of the family about my experience. José was never prosecuted, because of the criminal statute of limitations.

I was at home on a Friday afternoon in June of 2002, helping my son clean his room, when the phone rang. It was Fr. Clete Kiley, an official from the United States Conference of Catholic Bishops (USCCB). He asked if I would be willing to come to Dallas, Texas, and speak to the assembled bishops about my experience. I asked how he knew about me and he told me that the (then) bishop of Juneau, Michael Warfel, had recommended me to the President of the USCCB, Bishop Wilton Gregory. I agreed to come to Dallas and Fr. Kiley told me that the USCCB would take care of my airfare, meals and hotel costs. I was to fly to Dallas the following Wednesday and would speak on Thursday. He told me to try to keep the news to myself, as the USCCB was concerned that the survivors who were invited to speak would be hounded by the press before our presentations. He told me that of course I could share the news with family and close friends.

I called my sister and asked if she could tell the rest of the family, and we told Charles's parents. The entire meeting was going to be televised on C-Span, because of the huge impact the news of the clergy sexual-abuse crisis had caused in the United States. I was to speak before the assembled 300 bishops, the staff, and the press who would be present: a total of about 1000 people. I called my therapist, Nancy, and my friend Jeanie and our friends and neighbors Ed and Betsy. Ed was working for the Juneau *Empire* at the time and I stressed to him that I was telling him as a friend, and not a reporter. He asked if he could put his reporter hat on and asked if, when I was done with my presentation, I could call him and give him an interview. I promised that he would be the first interview I gave.

I flew to Dallas, accompanied by Bishop Warfel, who was kind and attentive during the trip. We arrived in Dallas and took a shuttle to our hotel, the Dallas Fairmont, certainly the nicest and most luxurious hotel I had ever been in! I was greeted by a lovely flower arrangement in my room from my sister Mary. It had a note with one word written on it: "Courage."

I was so nervous, I couldn't eat. At dinner time, I went to the dining room and looked at the menu. The only thing that appealed to me was a small shrimp salad. A nice bishop came and asked if he could sit with me. He introduced himself as Bishop Michael Pfeifer from San Angelo, Texas. He asked if that was all I was going to eat and urged me to eat more than just a small salad. I told him that I was so nervous about my presentation the next day that I couldn't eat any more. He said: "How about dessert then? Young man [gesturing to a waiter] do you have ice cream and cake?" I assured him that I really wasn't hungry for dessert (very unusual for me) and thanked him for his kindness. He then gave me a small Holy Spirit medal (which I still wear today) and gave me a blessing for the next day.

The next day, I arrived in the huge conference room and Bishop Warfel met me and took me around the room to meet as many bishops as he could introduce me to. All the bishops were very kind and encouraging.

After I gave my presentation, I took a few minutes to go to my room and recover a bit. I called Ed and gave him the promised interview, then all four of the survivors who spoke were given the opportunity to speak to the press. I was interviewed by the *New York Times*, the *Washington Post*, the *Dallas Morning News* and *USA Today*.

Then we were invited to watch the bishops as they worked on establishing the "Charter For The Protection of Children and Young People," a huge document that would become the guideline for dioceses in the United States. At one point, one bishop was arguing against having stipulations that a single offense would mean removal from the priesthood. I was sitting in the observer's section and I stood while he was speaking and remained standing until the bishops voted down his amendment, then I crossed myself and sat down.

Speaking in Dallas changed me profoundly. I used to be afraid of speaking in front of groups of people. I am no longer afraid. I used to be afraid to tell people about my experience of being abused—so much so that I was hesitant to join a support group of survivors because, as I told my therapist, "I can't talk about this in front of people." I used to feel powerless and helpless. Now I am strong. Speaking in Dallas was a healing experience, and while I am not happy for the reason that I was selected to speak, I am glad that I was given the opportunity to share my story.

While I was still in Dallas, Bishop Warfel asked me if I would serve on our diocesan Review Board. He said that my experience as a survivor gave me a unique perspective and that I would be a valuable asset to him and the board. I agreed, not knowing what was to come.

In November 2002, while Charles and I were at a conference in New York City, I received a call from my son, telling me that our pastor (Charles's boss at our parish) had been accused of child molestation by a young man. When we returned home, the pastor had been suspended from his duties pending a police investigation, which was requested by Bishop Warfel, even though the alleged offenses were not within the statute of limitations. The Review Board met several times, we listened to the testimony of the alleged victim, and because the news media had reported on the case, several other young men came forward with similar stories of misconduct, although none of them reached the level that the first accuser alleged. After many weeks, the Review Board advised Bishop Warfel to send the case to Rome and request that the priest be removed from the priesthood. The Vatican agreed that the offenses perpetrated against the original accuser were not provable, but because there were so many victims with similar accusations, and because the priest admitted to those offenses, he would be removed from the priesthood.

This experience had a huge effect on our family. Because we were so involved in our parish—Charles as the Director of Religious Education, and myself as a liturgical minister, with our children still involved in Religious Education—and because I was a Review Board member, we were confronted with the scandal in our parish on a daily basis. Parishioners whom I had known for more than 20 years, feeling that our pastor had been unjustly accused, refused to speak to me, saying that I had a personal grudge against priests and that I had urged our pastor's removal out of spite. As an example of the huge blind spot that several of our parishioners had about our pastor, our son, along with his fellow students in his religious education class, was asked by his catechist (who was a supporter of the pastor) to write a card of support to the priest. My husband, as DRE, immediately put a stop to that! Some people left the parish and moved to the other parish in our town. Some people left the Church completely, including several members of the diocesan Review Board.

During this period of upheaval in our family, our local parish, our diocese and the Catholic world, I was also meeting with the Benedictine religious superior of my abuser, to tell what José had done to me and the effect it has on my life. I asked them to publicly announce that he had been credibly accused and to take steps to have him removed officially from the priesthood. I met with them several times over the course of months to negotiate these requests. The abbot sent me a check for $5,000 to offset the expense of traveling back and forth from Alaska to Oregon. At one meeting, I was interviewed by members of their Review Board, who told me that they were not planning to make any public announcements because it would "ruin the life" of my abuser, and that by leaving active ministry and marrying, he had removed himself from the clerical state anyway. They also mentioned that they were concerned about the Abbey being sued by my abuser for slander. They showed me the abuser's signature on a letter he had written to the abbot, but they wouldn't let me read his letter. They also mentioned the money that the abbot had sent me, asking me if I didn't think that this payment was "enough," and if I couldn't just let it go.

I had never, since being molested by the abuser himself, felt so victimized and powerless. During the course of my life since the abuse, I had felt suicidal and desperate only a few times. This was one of those times. I sat in the rented car and sobbed. Obviously, I was not going to get any help from the Abbey, except a large check, which I didn't ask for in the first place.

The clergy sexual abuse crisis has affected every facet of my life: my childhood and adolescence, my life as a young single woman, my marriage, my parenting, and my spiritual life.

The Church has made many mistakes: from several popes who did not act on a global level to address the problem of clergy sexual abuse; to bishops, archbishops and cardinals who either ignored reports of child sexual abuse or, if they did take them seriously, moved the offenders to another parish; to parish priests, who, while innocent of any personal wrongdoing, turned a blind eye to the actions of their fellow pastors; to parishioners, who either did not believe that the problem existed or who blamed the victims for the resultant lawsuits and scandal.

I have been asked many times why I remain a faithful Catholic. I could never leave the Church. She is my family, and just like in any family, there are bad people and good people. I tend to celebrate the good people, try to forgive the bad ones, and just keep going. I have said many times that I will never leave the Church—the Church is going to have to throw me out. I am not meek; I speak my mind when necessary, as I have more than adequately demonstrated!

The main reasons I stay are because of Catholic social teaching, which guides and informs my life, and because of the sacraments, which nourish me. I am a daughter of the Church, and as flawed and broken as she is, I love her.

On Holy Thursday of 2016, the faithful of our Diocese were informed that a priest assigned to one of our local parishes had engaged in sexual harassment and propositioning of women in his parish. Our bishop removed him from active ministry and held a listening session for parishioners. He also instituted a yearly Ceremony of Sorrow to acknowledge the harm done to individuals who have been harmed by a representative of the Catholic Church.

I experienced the news that a priest was accused and admitted to such acts as a trigger and had flashbacks to my own experience. Other women spoke to me, saying that they too had been abused and were suffering from distress. As a follow up to the bishop's listening session and the Ceremony of Sorrow, several women, including myself, formed a compassionate listening group called RUaH, which stands for Reconciliation, Understanding and Healing.

The group, which is open to both men and women, meets regularly to share our stories of sexual, physical, and emotional abuse by representatives of the Church. We start with Scripture followed by a period of silent contemplation and reflection. Then, as each person wishes, they take an object in their hands (we use a rock or geode) to signify that they wish to speak. Then they share their story. The other participants listen intently and compassionately, offering no comment or crosstalk. Then, when the individual has finished talking, they replace the object on the table and we observe a period of silence to absorb and process what they shared. Then, the next person shares, until all who wish to speak have done so. At the end of the session, we together say the "Prayer for Healing Victims of Abuse," published by the United Conference of Catholic Bishops' Committee for the Protection of Children and Young People after their 2002 meeting:

> God of endless love,
> ever caring, ever strong,
> always present, always just:
> You gave your only Son
> to save us by his blood on the cross.
>
> Gentle Jesus, shepherd of peace,
> join to your own suffering
> the pain of all who have been hurt
> in body, mind, and spirit
> by those who betrayed the trust placed in them.
>
> Hear the cries of our brothers and sisters
> who have been gravely harmed,
> and the cries of those who love them.
> Soothe their restless hearts with hope,
> steady their shaken spirits with faith.
> Grant them justice for their cause,
> enlightened by your truth.
>
> Holy Spirit, comforter of hearts,
> heal your people's wounds
> and transform brokenness into wholeness.

Grant us the courage and wisdom,
humility and grace, to act with justice.
Breathe wisdom into our prayers and labors.
Grant that all harmed by abuse may find peace in justice.
We ask this through Christ, our Lord. Amen.[1]

RUaH has been a blessing to the individuals who have participated in the listening circles. My hope and prayer is that more individuals will be able to experience the peace that comes from being listened to with compassion and love, from being validated and believed, and that all of us who have been harmed will be fully healed from our pain. I encourage anyone who would like to know more about RUaH to contact me at the following address: ikon@ alaska.net.

1. "A Prayer for Healing Victims of Abuse," United States Bishops Conference, http://www.usccb.org/issues-and-action/child-and-youth-protection/resources/upload/Bilingual-PC.pdf.

You Say, This Is Not Poetry

Zach Czaia

You Say, This Is Not Poetry[1]

You say, this is not poetry:
The mother didn't understand how the boy could have
learned about sex already
No, it is a mother's hell. Hell is not a metaphor.
Curtis Wehmeyer kept his white 2006 camper parked
outside Blessed Sacrament Church
Several times, he touched one of the boys
You say, this is an old story. It is not poetry. Poetry is
meant to nourish the spirit. This kills it,
friend. We do not want to hear
That hope died last summer
When one of the boys told his aunt what happened in the camper
No, we want to know how to live.
We want the
"Nothing, nothing, nothing in this man's behavior known to us . . ."
To be true, to ring like a bell.
But it doesn't. It is a bad bell
and does not ring. It is hollow and without music.

---

1. The lines in italics are from the September 23, 2013, Minnesota Public Radio news story reported by Madeleine Baran. The lines in quotation are from former vicar general of the archdiocese of Saint Paul and Minneapolis, Father Kevin McDonough.

Memories of Father X

i.

In school, on church days, I was a reader,
hovered over the microphone and the big red book.
I was darkness over the deep. Though in my teenage bones
there was light as well as darkness.
Sometimes from the epistles of Paul, sometimes stories
of kings and prophets, never the words of Jesus—
property of the priest, his to say.
When I read, I dressed in robes like the boys
on the altar, and bowed like them before the altar.
I watched my friend hold another big red book
in front of the priest and felt sorry for him—
always Father X with his breath in the morning,
like an animal had lain overnight in his mouth and died
and death poured out his mouth along with the gospel.

ii.

Death poured out his mouth along with the gospel,
teeming with its interest for life. The blood
of Christ in the cup, raised, and my friends
on the altar ringing their bells at the priest's raising
of the cup and all of us staring.
                              Communion, the golden tray
beneath our chins to catch the crumbs of Christ, our tongues
extended to the host like waves, licking God
then lapping back to rejoin the sea, our seats
on the altar. Then songs in Latin, a prayer chanted back
and now we are on our feet with Father X,
processing down the aisle past classmates,
a riverboat in shallow waters of smirking,
hoping the girls forget that we have worn these robes,
that we have rung these bells.

iii.

And hoping the girls forget
we wore those robes and rang those bells,
we pass back to our seats in class, remembering Father X,
his shining nose, his sermon on The Rock
and what The Rock was cooking
and how we knew now he'd watched him wrestle,
the body oiled and gleaming for the television screen—
how he spoke, how he boomed, how the
shiver and shake of his voice
was like a storm brewing, how we loved the boom—
and how she sits, our crush,
like a sphinx in winter, winter-sphinx with
a thousand secrets riddled up inside her,
skirt rolled up to the very gates.

iv.

Skirt rolled up to the very gate,
she walks in beauty, like the afternoon,
sleepy seventh hour and nothing but time and Byron's poem,
the windows elsewhere only, and the frosted glass here,
just permeable enough to give the view:
Father X in full cassock astride the narrow hall like a Goliath.
Do you want a pass from out of class, he asks.
Is seventh a good time to talk?
The minute hand sweats its way forward, gropingly.
The dust crawls atop the radiator's back.
I finger my crush's gum underneath the Bunsen burner,
the spit and stickiness and will to stay close. Yes and yes.
With a word I'm stuck, hang and touch again, suspended
and hold the golden tray for all those tongues extended.

What I Am Most Angry About

What I am most angry about, Father X,
is something you couldn't control—
not a touch, not a word, not sex.
No. That you did your job, that I laid bare my soul,
that it lay naked before you, raw and clean:
a good kid in the flesh in the confessional.
Let me remember it, let me say what I mean.
The day before, on the way to football practice
a friend and I walking down Dale Street.
Old story: lineman complaining to his quarterback,
thought the coaches treated me special,
said something about one of them sucking my dick.
It was nothing personal. It was not unusual,
locker talk on the way to the field, a joke in passing,
but there I was in the middle of an image
and the coach he'd made suck it was a good one.
He taught me to tell zone from man,
how to fake a hand-off, how a huddle is run.
The throwaway line from my lineman
bothered me, kept me up all night.
That was my coach and I cared about him.
I had no girl and I cared about him. Did that make me gay?
That's where you came in, Father X.
A scared and wondering eighteen-year-old the next day
brought his worry in to confess.
You told him to pray to the Virgin Mary
if impure thoughts put him to the test.
They did not. The days went on as before.
The boy became a man. He fell in love.
He is not worried about this memory anymore.
He has forgiven you what you hadn't thought of
confessing: listening to a boy's worry.
He has forgiven you. It is enough

for now, this forgiveness in the third person.
He has thought about it a while
and it's all he can give now, nursing
as he still is some anger
but grateful mainly for escaping greater danger.

Discovering That I Am Beloved

"Casey"

I 'M NOT SURE I'M ready—but it's time to tell this story. Even if it's just for my own sake, it's time I understand the love story that is God's and mine.

I think the best place to start is with Christ's words of invitation that send a shudder of Holy Spirit chills down my spine every time I hear them: "He took the child by the hand and said to her, 'Talitha koum,' which means, 'Little girl, I say to you, arise!'"[1]

Growing up as the poster child for parochial education, I was the quintessential Catholic child. The dutiful eldest, I prayed methodically each night to Jesus to make me a saint. I devoured books on the greatest saints—and stuffed them under my bed during the scarier parts (the children of Fatima's vision of hell, St. Francis of Assisi's hair shirt, and Padre Pio's stigmata). I required ten minutes of wishing Jesus happy birthday before opening any Christmas gifts, and a penitential hour of dolorous play-time every Good Friday. I cried when cruel daylight savings time made me miss the opportunity to parade and celebrate Palm Sunday. And I tap-danced with glee on the church steps after my first Reconciliation.

These things were not instilled by my parents; they were the gift of a carefree childhood in which Christ was nothing but a hazy loving shepherd somewhere far above with his cloud-shaped sheep. I loved him, and I didn't need to know why. I was to be Jesus' most dutiful daughter. This was an ideal I mastered in childhood

---

1. Mark 5:41.

and abided by in my teen years with a heavy involvement in youth group and a regular Adoration hour.

I reached college relatively unscathed: no drinking, boy-friends, broken curfews, skipped Masses. Those things were just not in my nature. It was no deep virtue I had, but more a gratuitous gift in which life for me was easier and fuller the virtuous way. The temptations warned about in Scripture were an obscure myth I couldn't relate to. Throughout those years I felt esteemed as God's "best little daughter"—the term "best" superseding "little" and "daughter," of course. If you have a lovely childhood this vision of Christ seems suitable enough: the corny 1980s laughing Jesus painting, or the Jesus collage with faces from all over the world. It isn't until you experience the darkness of man that you must confront Christ on a deeper, sturdier level.

After I was raped my sophomore year of college, I was de-termined to let the Catholic faith I so heartily espoused in good times guide me in my time of strife. This was my opportunity to authentically live the gospel of redemptive suffering, which I had valued in the crucifix on my wall and the body and blood in my mouth—but not often in daily living. And because the ethereal Christ of clouds and laughs and crucifixes seemed so distant from my pain, I grasped for anything that could confirm my stalwart belief: God is good.

I met the best Catholic man. The daily Mass devotee, a regu-lar at Adoration. He was rumored to heal, speak in tongues, and prophesy. He made women cry, men kneel, priests overflow with praise . . . and the shrewd and prudent wary. He led the retreats, Bible studies, and prayer groups. As I lay rotting on an Adoration chapel floor, trying to be good, I only needed the charity of any passerby. And he was the one who saw me first.

What started as butterflies from an attractive religious man soon became a whirlwind of cultish superstition and worship of the most confused order. I soon became enamored with his com-pelling charisms and divine channel to God. He attended to me with his bandages of fake grace and the composure of religious superiority. A two-and-a-half-year relationship started in the simplicity and purity of courtship, group dates, and church events.

But I had never had a boyfriend before. I didn't know how this worked. I had never had a Catholic boyfriend; and as he was the holiest man I'd ever met, everything he deemed appropriate and judicious was somehow imprimatured by God himself in my eyes. This man who ministered the Eucharist at daily Mass each morning and took my pants off each evening, *this* was the man worthy of God's gifts.

It wasn't that I didn't hear the voices of nature and instinct crying out to me, pulling on my ear lobes, begging me to hear my own discomfort—it's just that it was easily overpowered by the rational well-measured arguments of the man before me. And so I did submit. Over and over again.

It was safely rationalized by being categorized in the "technically not sexual intercourse" category—even though we did everything but. And I never wanted to, but it just became easier to agree than endure his monologues. And when he compared my skills to those of his ex it resurrected in me a pained need for ownership over him. Eventually you forget who wanted it more in the first place, because it's as if he programmed you how he wanted.

I wasn't fit for God's spiritual gifts: the prophesy, the healing, the passion. Yet this man, him, *he,* had all of them. "WWJD?" was transformed into my new subconscious motto—"What would Thomas do?" I prayed only that I would be worthy of the man who became my boyfriend. I met Christ's mystery through the mastery of Thomas's hands. Through his spiritual prowess and gentle manipulation. He made God real. He made Christ a living breathing man. He was this anthropomorphic wonder, and yet existing in the small and ordinary modern day. There were miracles each moment with Thomas. The spiritual prowess and wonders I recalled in the hands of the apostles were something I believed reserved for the biblical time period, but Thomas embodied spiritual powers and authority that I knew only the apostles, Mary, and Christ have.

His shrewd eyes spotted everything. "See that guy waiting for the bus stop? I sense that he is battling some interior darkness."

And indeed when Thomas went to talk to him—he was.

"See this woman at the soup kitchen—the Spirit tells me she has had a traumatizing experience in a car"—and indeed, when he pressed her about it, she had.

"That man with arthritic pain—I believe I can heal him." And when he lay his hands on him, the man claimed to be healed.

But there was more than just the miracles. Thomas had a presence to offer. A charismatic, shepherding persona that people gravitated to.

"This young, attractive woman who just came back from a missionary trip to Mexico—she really needs me to help her process her experience. It's nothing more than that, I swear."

And his authority knew no bounds: "Casey, can you please wear a seatbelt. Casey, can you just trust and let go? Casey, you wouldn't need medicine and therapy if you were just trusting hard enough. Casey, I think I'm having the beginnings of stigmata. Casey, I wish you could be more like Mary. Don't hold my computer that way! I think this Lent we should give up physical stuff. Would you be open to trying oral? If you really let go . . . Casey, my crown of thorns is so painful now, should we call a priest? I think this Lent I'm only going to watch porn of married people. Casey, I offered up my meals for you today—for your healing. Casey, you are stifling yourself; if you just tried some of these things . . . I am not a bad man. Look into my eyes, don't you see Jesus' eyes? All these other women see Jesus' eyes. You don't? But oh Casey, you're not believing then. See, you still don't trust."

To recall it in retrospect, the narcissism, the evil, appears patent. But evil doesn't come clanging a gong. It starts slowly. It builds trust. It mingles with minute breakthroughs or reprieves from fighting to massage the scarring behavior out of your mind. Every physical boundary he encouraged me to break through, or helped me toss aside like a piece of clothing, was the work of repetition and days of wearing down. This loss of purity, he assured me, was a remnant from my rape. It eased the downward path of rejecting my virginal values, a path that led me to every physical activity save intercourse. It was his way of silencing Catholic teaching so he could sleep peacefully while I flopped in his covers rolling in guilt each night and feeling filthy each morning.

Then there was the one night. The one night he wanted to try something new. And I wasn't comfortable. I was unsure. But this was a different Thomas. One driven like a wolf by some alluring goal, some ruby, some flower. His eyes seemed different. Narrowed and focused. He walked around rabid, grabbing a roommate's condom and turning me over on his bed, freed by my tiniest gesture of submission. And then he sought what he wanted. And as I started crying in pain, some tiny unspoken "no" from years of subjection squeaked out. A "no" I lacked confidence in because I had never tried it before. Surely such a holy man listens to "no." No. I don't want this.

But he didn't listen. At least not at first. He continued his plunging, his treasure-seeking. And finally, so as not to be too barbaric, stopped and flopped down on the bed.

"Was it hurting? What's wrong?"

A week later he would laugh about it, "Remember when you cried like a little bitch?"

And I forgot about it and kept dating him for several more months.

Who was this Christ I devoted my life to? Does he not love his darling little girl? Does he gift an evil man with the Spirit and dismiss the small one crying in the bedroom corner?

I didn't encounter Christ for years after that. That's not to say I dropped my faith; a person can do a lot to practice their faith without *knowing* Christ. I graduated college, escaped to a convent and then escaped the convent. Lived with my parents. Went to therapy. I was no longer capable of encountering Christ interiorly but my actions would never reveal that. I devoutly prayed and cried to him daily—but always safely envisioning a mere tabernacle or an angry, bearded, God-of-Hosts. And I shook with fear of his love.

Terrified of any moment truly alone in a church. Terrified of lingering after a particularly emotional Mass. Terrified of encountering a strikingly holy person. Any silent secret moment that God peered through to grab my hand I quickly jerked away. So my healing with God was very difficult. And slow. Because you don't heal if you're picturing this God and not the Christ who scrubbed calloused feet, cried about a friend's death, and graciously accepted a perfume bath.

For many years I had met the distortion of love—the devil's greatest attacks on the greatest gift.

It has been six years and I long for some linear map of growth on how I've come to know Christ, but all I can say is I do know him—in a way, and there isn't *one way* to know him.

I think we all want that "burning bush moment." God speaking through the majesty of everyday objects to explicitly instruct and guide us through pain. But "Christ plays in ten thousand places, Lovely in limbs, and lovely in eyes not his."[2] For many sufferers of addiction or trauma I think coming to know Christ is something much more slow and painful.

It is a still small voice whispering hopes to a day of despair. It is wings of an angel lifting up the heavy arms of the depressed out of bed each day. It is sitting through a weekly Adoration hour despite paralyzing fear, and slowly, maybe after a year or two, it's the way that fear grows less.

It's having a cup of coffee with someone who understands your pain, and not being alone for an hour. It's pages of *A Story of a Soul* or *Interior Castle* read, an altar candle lit with hopeful purpose, an angry run in hateful zero-degree weather, an elderly woman in the chapel pulling Kleenex out of her purse. It's a random French monk grabbing your cheeks and telling you, "God loves you, damn it!"

It is your parents paying your way through therapy and their stolid tearful eyes following your unhealthy habits with precaution. It is hospital visits and trauma-induced migraines. It's a laugh, rusty after what seems like years of disuse, at Monty Python's *Life of Brian*. It's the hosts of angels and communion of saints pulling Christ's cloak on your behalf. It's praying, "Jesus, I want to know you, I *need* to know you," thirty-five times a day.

2. Gerard Manley Hopkins, "As Kingfishers Catch Fire," in *Poems and Prose* (Harmondsworth: Penguin, 1985).

It's a man who looks at you and your wreckage and asks you on a date. It's a marriage that answers every prayer you never even prayed, because it is just that loving. It is making it to today. It's the birds outside my window.

Christ sought me in all these ways. The days those men hurt me pierced wounds in my spirit, but that raw wound allowed a larger embrace and deeper healing from Christ. He saw that this little girl felt desertion and refused to be approached by him even in moments of prayer and he was so desperate to heal his daughter that he sought all possible ways. He is my father who loves me so profoundly he won't rush intimacy until I'm ready. And until then, he'll send me the birds.

I am not healed yet. There are still times I get nervous at a spiritual breakthrough. And I still interiorly battle a desire to ignore Christ beckoning to me. I spent my life, in many ways, with an imperfect, fractured knowledge of Christ. Tonight is another night where I will battle myself to open my heart up to the Lord I am growing to know. I will close my eyes in peace despite the struggle of understanding this mass of mystery. And I will dream nestled like a sheep upon his lap. And I will struggle to know he loves me. And tomorrow morning, as he does every morning, he will say to me, *"Talitha koum"*—"little girl . . . arise!"

Jesus Is Not an Abusive Boyfriend

"Elena"

THE DEPRESSION WAS BACK. Four years previous, I had been diagnosed with severe depression. I was basically nonfunctional. I got on meds, got myself to counseling, and managed to climb back out of the hole I had found myself in. But now, I couldn't deny that the black sticky tar of depression that held me down and suffocated me was creeping back. Praying in the chapel one day at Adoration, I felt deep in my heart a certainty that Jesus wanted me to go to confession. Normally I went every three or four months, and it hadn't been that long, but Jesus was insistent.

"Okay, I'll go," I said. "But what do I confess?"

"That you don't trust me," he said.

My parish didn't offer confession at any time that was convenient for me, so I looked online and found one that did. That next Tuesday evening, I drove up to St. Zita,[1] waited in line, and when it came to be my turn I entered the confessional.

I always go to face-to-face confession because the confessional screen was part of the abuse I experienced from a priest in my youth. But this time I didn't look up at the priest; I just started talking.

"Bless me father for I have sinned, I. . . well, just to give you some background, my dad was killed in a hunting accident when I was almost three and I've spent several years working through that loss in counseling. But I still don't trust God and I felt like I was supposed to come here and confess that."

1. All proper names have been changed to preserve confidentiality.

The priest spoke a few words of encouragement and then asked "Do you know who I am?"

I looked up at his face and didn't recognize him, but I had a feeling that meeting this priest was why God had specifically called me to confession here.

"Who is he?" I wondered. "Maybe he's some visiting priest who has written a book on grieving. Maybe he's a priest-psychologist who specializes in bereavement . . ."

But nothing could have prepared me for what he said next.

"I am the priest who buried your father," he said. "Father Bill. I remember you, a little three-year-old. I was pretty sure I recognized you as soon as I saw you come in but when you said 'hunting accident,' I knew that it was you."

I couldn't speak. This was why God wanted me to come here. He wanted me to have proof that he cared and that he was still at work in my life, that the story wasn't over yet.

As time went on, I came to realize that God hadn't just brought Father Bill back into my life for that one moment, but for the unraveling that was to come. God could not have been more clear if he had appeared in that confessional and said "This is your confessor. Listen to him, trust him."

I continued to confess to Father Bill every couple of months as he recommended. He was more insightful, more gentle, and more encouraging than any priest I had ever received direction from. The way he shepherded me in the name of Christ began to change my image of God.

The primary picture I had of God up until this point, though I would have denied it, was of someone who was all-powerful and had authority over me, but wanted to control me. Someone who demanded that I conform myself to his will. Basically, someone who abused his authority to use me for his own benefit, without considering me as a person with feelings that mattered.

My intellectual understanding of God and the church mainly came from the teachers and priests at a school that I attended which was run by a religious order, and then another "independent school in the Catholic tradition" after that.

My parents were loving and faithful Catholics, but the wound I received from my father's sudden death, which turned my life upside down, primed me to see God as someone who could abandon me at any moment, someone whose love and attention I had to earn while being constantly afraid that I wasn't good enough. I was also really afraid of death.

This wasn't helped by the religious figures at my schools. Here are some of the twisted things I was taught, which I believe constitute spiritual abuse:

"When St. Joan of Arc was asked if she was in the state of grace, she replied 'I hope so.' One can never know for sure if one is in the state of grace; that would be presumption. You never know, you might have mortal sin on your soul."

"St. Maria Goretti's motto was 'death rather than sin.'"

"You want to do penance and mortify yourself here on earth and not wait till Purgatory. Purifying ourselves in this life is like untying a knot. It's hard work, but persevere and it can be done. The purification of Purgatory is like ripping the knot apart. It's unbelievably painful. Confession and absolution forgives the eternal punishment due to sin, but the temporal punishment still remains. That's why it's important to get indulgences, plenary if you can—but that involves having no attachment to sin and basically no one can do that."

"Don't be lukewarm or God will spit you out of his mouth. Join the Movement [meaning, the order which ran the school and its affiliated group for laypeople] because you don't want to be a lazy Catholic."

"If you're not sure if something is a mortal sin, confess it anyway. Better to be safe than sorry. If you're not sure if you're in the state of grace, better to abstain from receiving Communion rather than committing sacrilege and 'eating and drinking condemnation upon yourself.'"

This was a view of the human person that exalted human willpower far beyond the reality. Mercy was given to others, but you could never expect it or count on it. The idea was that God gives everyone the grace to do what he calls us to do, and he calls us to be perfect—so any imperfection must be willful on my part and therefore a sin. If you said, "I can't do this," the only explanation was that you were being disobedient and rejecting God's grace.

We were taught to focus on others and not ourselves, which meant deferring to their wishes instead of our own. Our school emphasized obedience; not gossiping; and "purity," which meant not talking or thinking about anything remotely sexual. The rumor was that boys and girls had to have physical education class on different sides of the school building because the administrators didn't want the boys to see the girls stretching and running—that could be a "temptation" to them. I began to fear my body as something that would betray me and cause people to see me as a thing and not a person.

This environment fostered an unbelievable amount of perfectionism, fear, and all-or-nothing thinking in me, and I became quite scrupulous. I learned not to trust my judgment on anything but to allow the priests and others in authority to usurp the role of my conscience and the role of God in my life. I learned that if I followed the rules, made sure everyone in authority was happy with me, and identified with them completely in what they said and thought, I would be accepted. I would not be rejected or abandoned and I would be safe.

Leaving the "Angry Jesus" Behind

Depression and the realities of parenting four small children while in a challenging marriage severely tested these beliefs. I finally had to admit that I am incapable of following every rule, being perfect all the time, never making mistakes and never acting in ignorance; and that if God was someone who required the impossible of me then I didn't want to serve him anyway.

I remember one day in the chapel writing down all the things that "Angry Jesus" said to me. Upon rereading what I had written, I realized that my view of Jesus was more like an abusive boyfriend than a savior or a friend.

I had written,

Your sin is your own fault and I'll only forgive you if you don't do it again. No matter how good your intentions were, you should have known better. I'm just. I owe you nothing. You deserve Hell. I was testing you, you failed. You can do all things through Me. That means if you ever do something wrong, it's because YOU failed. I always give you "the grace" to do it, whatever that means. I always win this game, it makes me feel better about Myself. You have to believe everything the church teaches immediately, no hesitation, no questioning. Well, you can question, but there's not a whole lot of point because you KNOW what answer you have to get if you don't want Me to abandon you. I'll never abandon you—as long as you do what I want. Be perfect, like Me. Ohhhh, snap! You can't! Well, maybe if you're really, really, really good and nice to me I'll let you in to Heaven. But really, we both know what you really are—say it with Me now— NOT. GOOD. ENOUGH.

Oh, you thought that peace and acceptance you felt earlier was Me? Nah. That was your own delusion again. The truth hurts, baby. And the truth is, I've never loved you. I've taken care of you so I could still look good and be praised. I've given you just enough to keep you in line.

Even now, you writing all this? It's blasphemy. You're just making things worse for yourself. I'm going to demand even more groveling and penance and pain from you now before you can earn your way back into your prison of fear, er, I mean, into My good graces. But that's how you like it, isn't it. Because at least you can be sure. You know where we stand, you and I, and you understand this little game we play. You can't leave Me. You'll never find anyone as good as Me. Sometimes you suspect that I'M not really Jesus at all, that there is a being out there who placed these desperate yearnings in you and Himself yearns to satisfy them with Himself. Who doesn't care how broken or wounded you are, who doesn't need you to do anything except come to Him and who will never cast you out no matter how much you mess up.

> But you're too scared to take a chance and that's the way I like it. I own you and there's nothing you can do about it.

I stopped and reread what I had written. Then I wrote, in big block letters,

> THIS IS NOT THE VOICE OF GOD.
>
> THIS IS THE VOICE OF THE ACCUSER.
>
> I HAVE LISTENED FAR TOO LONG.
>
> I AM DONE.
>
> I LISTEN ONLY TO THE VOICE OF GOD, THE ONE TRUE GOD.
>
> If he is all-powerful and all-loving, he can and will make me hear His voice. And if not, then I don't want Him anyway. So who is God, really? Start with Ed [my husband]. God cannot be less loving, less forgiving, less generous, less accepting, less faithful than Ed.

That was the beginning of escaping the prison of fear that was built by spiritual abuse.

Sunlight

Through continued counseling and the support of a twelve-step group for codependents, I slowly grew into myself. It wasn't until at least a year of meetings (and several years of counseling) that I had developed enough of a healthy sense of boundaries to begin to understand that what the priest did to me in the confessional at age twelve was definitely not okay. Before this point, I kept telling myself that I must have been missing something, and that somehow his intentions must have been good. We learned in my group that denial is a protective mechanism that our mind uses when we are not yet capable of dealing with a particular truth. I was definitely in denial. I recognized that these things would have clearly been abusive if they had been done to someone else, but was sure that somehow in my case it couldn't have possibly been abuse—because that would mean that I had been abused by a priest in the confessional and I couldn't deal with that.

When the news came out about Josh Duggar molesting his sisters, I happened upon a blog written by women who had been groomed and abused by an older, religious authority figure. In their stories I recognized mine. I recognized that none of it just "happened," but that it was all planned by this man who was a predator. I realized that twelve-year-olds, especially ones already in an environment that values absolute obedience and discourages discussing anything negative about anyone else (this was labeled "gossip" and "uncharitable"), are not equipped to recognize the advances of a sexual predator or to respond as an adult would.

Around the same time, a college friend of mine who is now a priest and a canon lawyer overheard me saying something about a priest being inappropriate with me and strongly encouraged me to report the incidents.

"Sunlight is the best disinfectant," he said. "And I have no sympathy for priests who take advantage of children like this. They make my job ten times harder."

This was *not* what I had expected to hear from a priest—I had expected to be chastised for "gossip" and asked to not talk about it.

A few years after I first started confessing to my confessor (the one God sent me, remember?) I decided to mention that I had been abused to him and to my counselor. They both strongly encouraged me to report it as well. After several weeks of wrestling with it (and weeks of emotional support for which I will be ever grateful to my college friend, Father Tom, who first reached out to me) I called my diocese and said that I needed to report past abuse of a minor by a priest.

After a conversation with the diocesan representative, I was told that I would need to bring my allegations directly to the religious order, because my abuser had been a member of their congregation and the diocese does not have canonical jurisdiction over religious orders. She directed me to the order's head of Safe Environment Accreditation. I felt sick when I heard who he was.

There had been two priests at the school the year I was abused: my abuser—and the priest who was now their Safe Environment Coordinator.

I called Father Tom in tears, asking what I could do. He said that it would be completely reasonable for me to request a contact in the order with whom I had no personal history. I did, and they assigned someone else to my case, but I still had to meet with them.

Through God's providence, a friend of my family is a lawyer and a devout Catholic. He agreed to accompany me to the meeting and, when the diocese said we couldn't meet in their pastoral center, offered the use of his conference room. Having him there was *huge* for me. Here was someone on my side, finally.

I felt like the diocese kind of washed their hands of me once they found out my abuser wasn't a diocesan priest, and I didn't trust the religious order at all. I felt like I was walking into a trap going into the meeting. Here were the people who not only created an environment for abuse but somehow warped my mind so that I didn't say anything for twenty years. I felt like I would crumble before them. So having my family friend there with me made me feel like I had a champion who wanted to protect me.

Reporting Abuse: You're on Your Own

I am really disappointed with the process in the diocese. This order is here in the diocese by the bishop's permission, and still operates that school by his permission. If I had called and said that I was pregnant and didn't know if I could keep my baby, or that I was an immigrant who needed citizenship classes, or that I needed a food pantry, there are ministries for that. Yet there was nothing for me. They wouldn't even release the letter they wrote to Child Protective Services about my allegations to me, citing legal reasons.

The pro-life ministry here has a program called Project Gabriel, where mothers in crisis pregnancies can be paired with a "Gabriel Angel," a woman who has been trained to be a source of support and encouragement for the pregnant mother. Parishes all over the diocese have Stephen Ministers, who are there to minister to people who are bereaved or grieving. Why is there nothing to help victims of abuse when they first report it?

I am fortunate that I had friends who are priests and canon lawyers who I was able to talk to and get information on how the process of reporting abuse within the Church would go. Many people do not have these connections.

Healing My Soul: Liturgy and Adoration

About the time that I was reporting the abuse, I started to get panic attacks during Sunday Mass. I would start to feel anxious and trapped around the homily, and by the consecration I would be in tears. If I wanted to be able to stay in the church for the entire Mass and not run out, I had to take so much Xanax before Mass that I would be a zombie for hours afterward. If I didn't take the Xanax, the stress of going to Mass would drain me so much that when I got home I would have to sleep for a few hours.

I talked to Father Tom about this and he said that the Sunday obligation is not binding if we are not able to fulfill it, and that could very well be the situation I was in. Another friend suggested I look into a Mass that would be different enough from what I was used to that it would not trigger my anxiety, like a Mass in a different language or a different rite. I decided to visit the Byzantine Catholic Church the next Sunday and for the first time in months, I did not have an anxiety attack or panic during Mass at all. I felt like Jesus had made a safe place for me to still be with him through his Church but without all the traumatic memories.

As I continued to attend Divine Liturgy (Mass) there I realized that God was not only giving me a safe space away from memories of abuse but that he was also answering my prayer to be re-catechized without the spiritual abuse, because Byzantine theology is expressed so differently even though they teach the same truth of the Catholic faith.

I don't know what is going to happen next. I don't know if I will ever be able to attend a Roman rite Mass again. I do know that I ran to the Byzantines for shelter and I ended up falling in love with their expression of the faith—the language, the art, the chanting—and the particular sense of community and family this parish offers, and it is my spiritual home now.

At one point in the process I also started to feel angry with the priest who had abused me. And then I felt very, very scared. I was picturing Jesus standing over me, accusing me of having such violent thoughts toward one of his priests. I felt like Jesus must be on *his* side.

Then I realized, believing that Jesus was on the priest's side was part of the lie. I imagined how angry I would be if someone hurt one of my children. Pretty angry. Then I imagined how angry I would be if someone hurt one of my children *and told them that I was okay with them being hurt.* That I knew about it, was in on it, had planned it. That was more than anger, that was rage.

And then I realized, the *only* reason this man wasn't struck dead the moment he touched me is because God's mercy is as great as his justice.

And somehow knowing that God was on my side, that he was just as angry as I was, helped me to find forgiveness alongside the anger. I will not stay quiet for fear of getting this man in trouble, but I will hope that no matter what trouble my honesty causes for him, it will bring him to a point where he can get right with God and know how much God loves him.

There have been times when the image I had of God was so twisted that I couldn't even call upon the name of God in prayer. In these moments the twelve-step idea of God as Higher Power who cares for us was very helpful. And no matter what I called God, he answered.

I have always loved Eucharistic Adoration because it was time with just me and Jesus, face to face. Quality time is my "love language" so this makes sense. I have continued to try to spend some quiet time in the chapel weekly, usually journaling while I pray.

The other thing I like about the Eucharist is that I don't need any words. No one can twist the words that aren't spoken. In communion I let Jesus into the inmost part of my heart, and that is only space for him and me. The abusers controlled my actions and played on my fears, but they did not enter into my heart of hearts. That is for God and me alone.

I try to go to confession every two months to Fr. Bill. I feel like he understands what I struggle with and what I need. One time my penance was to think of some positive quality about myself and then thank God for giving me that quality, and to know that I am his beloved daughter with whom he is well-pleased. He actually encourages my relationship with God, instead of trying to get in the middle of it and take the place of God, which is spiritually abusive.

One thing that has really helped me distinguish God's voice from others is something that Pope Benedict XVI said: "Josef Pieper, in his book on love, has shown that man can only accept himself if he is accepted by another. He needs the other's presence, saying to him, with more than words: it is good that you exist."[2] If someone starts to try to convince me to believe or think a certain way, I ask myself if they are starting from the premise that I am good—that it is good that I exist. If not, I don't even have to listen to them, because what they are saying is not true. I've told God this too, that anything he wants to say to me has to start with, "It is good that you exist, Elena." If it doesn't, I will assume it's not from him.

At the school run by the religious order there was a lot of fear surrounding discerning God's will and making the right choices. I felt like if I had questions or was unsure about God's will for me then I simply wasn't listening hard enough. There was a line in the recent movie *Noah* where Methuselah (Anthony Hopkins) says to his grandson Noah (Russell Crowe), "You must trust that the Creator will speak to you in a way you can understand."[3]

This was eye-opening to me. God is perfectly able to communicate with me in a way that I can understand. If I am genuinely

2. Pope Benedict XVI, "Address of His Holiness Pope Benedict XVI on the Occasion of Christmas Greetings to the Roman Curia," Clementine Hall, Vatican City, December 22, 2011.

3. Darren Aronofsky and Ari Handel, *Noah* (DVD), directed by Darren Aronofsky (Los Angeles: Paramount Pictures, 2014).

seeking his will for me and seeking to draw nearer to him, that is all he needs. He can do the rest. If I ask and am still confused, if I try to draw near but still feel far away, then for some reason in his grace and his plan he is allowing me to stay in ignorance or to stay unaware of his presence for the time being.

Even though I have been hurt very badly by Catholics, some acting in the name of the Church, so far every time that I've felt like I have to leave the Church to get away from those who hurt me, God has put *good* Catholics in my path. They are a sign to me that I don't have to leave the Church to save my sanity; that I can be me and still be Catholic.

I believe Christ founded the Church and that the Holy Spirit guides it. I believe that Christ is present in the sacraments, most especially in the Eucharist. Even so, I would not be able to stay if all I encountered in other Catholics and in the institution of the Church was condemnation, abuse, lies. . . . I still have to work hard not to fall back into that pattern of abdicating my selfhood and my responsibility to someone else who wants to play God in my life. If that was all I encountered in the Church, I would have to leave in order to be free of these unhealthy behaviors.

I am grateful that Jesus has made a way for me to stay, to be able to reject those false ideas about God without having to reject the Church. I still have to constantly work to separate the two.

I don't pray the rosary. It brings up too many feelings of performing actions for God's approval. One of the things I did when I was involved with the religious order's school was commit to saying a decade of the rosary every day. So it still has some bad associations for me. I am learning to draw closer to Mary as the Theotokos (God-bearer, or colloquially, "birth-giver to God") since she is mentioned multiple times in the Divine Liturgy (what Byzantines call Mass).

I don't wear religious jewelry. People used my faith and the things I loved to manipulate me and hurt me, so I don't share my faith unless I trust the person I am talking to. I have my own symbols and reminders that don't mean anything to anyone else. One necklace I have with a Pac-Man charm reminds me to pray for and with my dad who passed away. Another necklace with a feather charm and an arrow reminds me that God is my protector. I guess you could say these are my sacramentals.

I'd like to be able to wrap this up into a nice, neat conclusion and tell you that I've resolved all my mistaken views of God and feel safe again within the Catholic Church. But I can't. I'm still working through things, I still get a lot of anxiety in the Roman rite Mass, I'm still angry with my abuser and with all those who enabled him.

The most helpful thing, and what I have come to believe God wants from me most of all, is to be real with him. Not to pretend I trust him or always like him or to make sure to say all the right prayers, but to be honest with him. Even if that means telling him that I'm not sure I trust him. Jesus comes to meet us where we are, and *where we are* is the only place we'll find him. If I pretend to be in a different place spiritually or emotionally than I really am, I'll miss an encounter with him.

This is very humbling because often I don't like the place where I am, I feel like I should be better, should be further along in the healing process, should trust more, should, should, should. But I have to choose—do I want to have a high opinion of myself for being so spiritually mature, or do I want to be loved for who and what I am? I want to be loved.

Part II: The New Village Church

The second part explores the ways in which our churches are smaller than they might seem. How can we learn to live together, honoring our differences instead of being divided by them? Social media has brought back the old village gossip; and words and deeds that might seem trivial or harmless turn out to have far-reaching ripple effects. We are truly one body—even when we might not want to be.

Dana Cunningham gives a family history, a memoir of black Catholic life in Texas from the civil rights movement to the death of Trayvon Martin. She reminds us that the days of burning crosses and segregated churches are not far behind us. But what begins as a story of the past's poison seeping into the present becomes a depiction of the urgency and difficulty of forgiveness. It is only forgiveness, Cunningham reminds us, that can bind our churches together.

Joanne Butler gives a punchy, fast-paced tale of financial misconduct in the Diocese of Arlington, Virginia, and offers an extremely practical solution (lay finance councils) as well as a cultural corrective (lay Catholics need to start caring where their money goes).

Rachel LaPointe writes about her decision to "parish-shop" after her former parish made her feel unwelcome for having a big family and refusing to hide the fact that she received government benefits for them.

M. Saverio Clemente, a doctoral student in philosophy at Boston College, offers an Augustine-influenced essay about bad catechism classes, self-righteousness, and protecting one's loved ones without becoming prideful. Clemente describes his cousin's experience of being treated as "less-than" by their neighbors and fellow parishioners because he had been born out of wedlock. Clemente found that his anger at these judgmental neighbors was damaging his own spiritual life. When he returned to his faith after a period of wandering, he had to let go of the anger and acknowledge his own sins.

Sarah reflects on losing her hearing in adulthood. That change has made it hard to find a parish where she can participate fully in the Mass—but it's also introduced her to the culture, community, and faith of Deaf Catholics.

Memories of a Black Catholic Childhood

Dana Cunningham

I AM A LIFELONG CATHOLIC. My mother's family was from Louisiana. Her great-grandparents and older ancestors were Catholics from Louisiana, who moved to Texas so that their children could get a better education. All my life I have been guided and sheltered in the Catholic Church—and all my life I have had to fight against racism, even in our churches. Learning to meet hatred with love has been one of the great spiritual battles of my life.

I was born in 1947 and raised in Beaumont, Texas; I attended segregated schools until I left for college.

Beaumont was a sleepy river town with farms and merchants until the Spindletop gusher brought the oil boom. My Grandpa Sprott moved to Beaumont then, along with hundreds of others, chasing "black gold." The land is flat and the Neches River runs along the downtown. There are shipyards and a huge Mobil Oil refinery south of downtown, bordering one of the black neighborhoods, the South End. There are oil fields south of town with pumps and huge, round oil storage tanks spotting the land. My grandfather Babino worked at the smaller Pure Oil refinery in Nederland. The Gulf Oil refinery in Port Arthur is even larger than Mobil. Now there is a DuPont chemical plant west of the town. So the local industries are oil, petrochemicals, shipping, rice farming and cattle (further west). The weather is hot and humid most of the year. It's said that the humidity can be 99 percent without it raining. When I was growing up there was very little air-conditioning, and we had window fans, or paper fans to try to keep cool. The windows were open most of the time, in hopes of catching a breeze. Afternoon rains gave us a little respite, but just created more steam when the sun came out.

I received my Catholic education at Our Mother of Mercy Parish in the Pear Orchard neighborhood, which was one of two parishes for African-Americans in Beaumont. These parishes were warm, loving communities of faith. My older family members were devout Catholics and attended daily Mass. My great-great grandmother, Agatha Richard Babineaux, lived on the property of Blessed Sacrament Parish, worked for the priests, and greeted the schoolchildren each morning.

I have fond memories of going to different homes in my grandmother's neighborhood for rosaries and novenas, adding special prayers for those who were ill, or having difficulties. When I was a preteen I joined the Sodality along with other girls in the parish. We wore white dresses and blue capes and had weekly meetings and participated in the procession once a month at Mass. CCD classes (the Confraternity of Christian Doctrine, or religious education for Catholics) were held on Tuesdays and Thursdays for those who didn't attend Catholic school. We memorized *all* the questions and answers in the Baltimore Catechism: "Who made me? God made me to know Him and love Him and serve Him in this world and the next."

After catechism my brothers and I would walk to Grandmother's for a snack. She always had something delicious on the stove. Grandmother went to 5:30 a.m. Mass on Sundays and we also stopped by after we went to 10:00 a.m. Mass. Her dinner would be cooked so we had a small taste to hold us until we got home and our mother cooked our dinner. Mass and catechism are tied in my mind to visits with Grandmother and her good food.

There were annual church bazaars with game booths, religious goods and chicken dinners to raise money for the parish. The parish was not only the center of our spiritual life, but also a social center. We saw parishioners at school, at the pool, shopping. We were always well behaved when any of the adults were around, because we knew our parents would be told if anyone saw us when we were on our own.

Our churches had Knights of St. Peter Claver (founded by the Josephite Fathers) instead of Knights of Columbus. St. Peter Claver was a priest who worked with enslaved Africans in South America and is the patron saint of African-Americans.

Our Catholic life was fenced in and shadowed by the racism that surrounded us. Outside the black community we were not welcome and not safe—even from other Catholics. When we attended Mass at the white parishes in Beaumont, we had to sit or stand at the rear of the church and couldn't go to the Communion rail to receive the Eucharist. It made me feel isolated from the rest of the congregation and as if I was not as worthy to fully participate and receive Christ at the table of the Lord as the rest of the congregation. I could not be as fully engaged and embraced in the body of Christ as I was at my home parish.

My grandmother, great-grandmother, great aunts and two of my uncles were the most faithful Catholics I knew. My great-aunt and her cousin were nuns, Handmaids of Mary. When I was five years old my mother took my two brothers and me to New York to visit Mother Eugenia and Sister Cecilia at the convent in New York. My mother had lived in the convent with the nuns while she attended college. While we were there I was thrilled to be a flower girl at the final vows for the young nuns who were becoming "Brides of the Church." It was like a wedding ceremony and I got to wear a beautiful ruffled dress and flowers in my hair.

But why were the Handmaids in New York? Their convent was originally in the South, before being chased away by the Ku Klux Klan and relocating to Harlem and Staten Island in New York. I heard my grandmother talk about how frightened she was for her sister and how they worried until they knew she was safe in New York.

My mother drove us to school, but we took the public buses home. Blacks had to sit in the back of the bus, but we started sitting wherever we liked. We attended meetings at a Congregational church in the North End that had a white minister. At the meetings we were trained in non-violence in anticipation of taunts and even attacks while demonstrating. We were anxious to be a part of the movement, and used the time between transferring to our next bus to sit-in at the lunch counter at Walgreen's. We were not served, but we didn't encounter any of the hateful behavior that we saw on television that other demonstrators endured.

I was in junior high school during the civil rights movement. My parents emphasized to us that we could not judge people by the color of their skin. Good and bad people come in all colors, and we were to judge each person as an individual. My father's oldest brother, Ed Sprott, MD, was the president of our local NAACP and all the adult men that we knew met and developed strategies to improve things in our community. Ed was very outspoken and always wrote letters to the editor of the newspaper. I remember Adam Clayton Powell and other national NAACP lawyers coming to our house for a meeting with representatives from the branches in neighboring towns.

It was all very exciting and fun to be a part of something so big—until one night, when bombs were thrown at our house, at my uncle Ed's house, and at the hospital that he built to serve the African-American community because he and the other black doctors were denied privileges at the white hospitals.

Now it all became very frightening. We knew that there were people who didn't want us to eat at lunch counters or restaurants, try on clothes at the department stores, use the public library, attend schools with white kids. Now they knew where we lived and they meant us harm. Fortunately, the bombs didn't do any serious damage to the properties. But seeing the homes of other civil rights leaders bombed or burned, and knowing that Medgar Evers had been killed in his own driveway, showed us that this was serious business.

Our priests were Josephite Fathers, white priests whose mission was to serve African-American parishes. They were very supportive of the movement, but we knew that not all the priests and nuns were.

Beaumont was segregated with three black neighborhoods—the North End, South End and Pear Orchard. My parents always wanted us to have the best teachers, so we changed schools and ended up going to schools all over town. The Catholic schools integrated when I entered the eleventh grade.

Texas colleges and universities were integrated in 1965, right after I finished high school. I was the valedictorian of my class and was awarded a scholarship to any Texas school, but I was not ready for the challenges of being the first black student at a previously all-white school. I chose the University of Denver, where my cousin from Chicago was enrolled. Family members vacationed in Colorado Springs each summer, so I knew it was scenic and besides, I would need a new wardrobe for the winters there. I met my husband who was attending the US Air Force Academy. We married after his graduation and have three children and three grandchildren. Our oldest son works for a game show company, the second son is a missionary priest, and our daughter works in social media.

We have lived in many places, and we've experienced many kinds of racism. It seems like the reminders are inescapable, even in church. In Arizona I used to attend Mass with a family whose children yelled racist taunts at my own children. They lived on our street and always sat in the first pew of the chapel, and were the first to receive Communion. I found it very difficult to be in the proper frame of mind to worship when I went to Mass and saw them front and center. So I stopped going to Mass for several weeks. Even when I tried to meet with a priest to share my feelings, I found that he harbored his own prejudices.

After several months, missing the church I had grown up in, I sought a new church, and found one that had a wonderful motorcycle-riding priest in leather boots. I'll never forget his sermon that All Saints Day. He spoke of the everyday saints that live among us and I could envision my great-grandmother, great-aunts and my grandmother. They went to Mass and prayed the rosary every day. They welcomed the poor and weary into their homes. They comforted those who needed comforting. They truly lived the gospel. I realized that they were the embodiment of the gospel and I should not let those who had gone astray keep me away from God's grace.

But it was hard for me to know how to cope with the persistent reminders that other Catholics did not see me as an equal, and did not take seriously my family's fight for freedom. At a parish staff meeting, another parishioner made a joke about the KKK. I kept silent at the time, but I tossed and turned all night as I thought of the violence inflicted on my family by the Klan, and of their sacrifices and struggles for justice. The next day I spoke with the jokester and told him that there was nothing funny about the Klan. I related how our home, my uncle's home, and the hospital he built to serve the black community had all been bombed by the Klan. His response was that he was just telling a joke and I should get over it, laugh and not be upset. What a kick in the gut! I walked away from him and wrote him off.

Shortly after that incident we had a program on the Lord's Prayer that was one of those life-changing experiences for me. It took the prayer phrase by phrase, starting with "Our Father . . ." and emphasizing that it says "*Our* Father," not "Father" or "my Father." The takeaway was that we are church, in community with each other, not just in a one-on-one relationship with God. That means that we are called to love each other—not just those who are easy to love, but all of God's people, even those who hate me. It was a lesson that I have not forgotten.

Years later, I attended a weeklong retreat in Tijuana, Mexico, where my younger son attended seminary with the Missionaries of Charity Fathers (the order founded by St. Teresa of Calcutta). My husband had recently had cancer surgery. Without knowing the focus of the retreat, the format, or anything else, I knew that I wanted to go to give thanks for my husband's successful surgery. It was a week long, with no phone, TV, computer, newspaper, etc. We slept on cots and ate very simple food. It was the first time in my life that I was free to focus entirely on my relationship with God without any distractions.

The Missionaries of Charity Mother House sits in a very poor, desert neighborhood in Tijuana, near the Otay Mesa. It is at the bottom of the mesa in an area that floods after heavy rains. On the grounds there is a chapel, a covered gathering space, a contemplative garden, classrooms, a beautiful courtyard with fruit trees and plants, small guest quarters, a kitchen and dining room, a hermitage, and living space for the priests and seminarians.

The retreat included a forgiveness session that had a profound impact on my life. All the retreatants gathered in a small room, sitting on the floor. A seminarian sat at the front of the room and read a long list that called to mind all the hurts that any of us could have suffered during our lives, from the womb to the present, including wounds from God, parents, self, friends, spouses, children, etc. Each statement that was significant for me stirred up a pain in my heart and in my gut as strong as when the initial hurt was felt.

We then went to a private space to record our personal hurts. I had struggled with forgiveness before, but this was definitely the first time I consciously reflected on it so deeply.

The next morning we were asked to pray for each person who was the source of pain, calling them by name and forgiving them. I was left with a physical reminder of the need to release hurt, anger, rancor and resentment so that I could be free to receive God's love—to be filled and immersed in *his* eternal love. It was a freeing experience that called to mind the movie title "The Incredible Lightness of Being." Letting go made me feel so light that I could have floated up to heaven.

When I forgive and let go, I become one with God again. I shared this with one family member who has a lot of anger about racial injustice. I told him he has to forgive. His reply was, "They haven't asked me to forgive them, and until they do, I can't forgive."

Then I get to these last few years and racism rears its ugly head in my current parish. It's easy to love and feel a bond with the "saints" in my parish, but quite a challenge to love the sacristan who referred to Mrs. Michelle Obama as an animal; or the usher who spoke derisively of Trayvon Martin and said that it should have been Barack Obama who was killed; or the very active church members who said I should just forget and move on after the nine people were killed in their church during Bible study in South Carolina.

That gut wrenching feeling of hurt and anger reappeared. I felt the pain of Trayvon Martin's mother and envisioned my sons at his age and my young grandsons. I thought of how easily they could have been frightened by being pursued by an unknown man and started running only to be shot to death. I thought of the pain of the families in Charleston, South Carolina, and the martyrdom of their loved ones. Reading the Facebook comments of a few parishioners following each incident made me wonder how many others in our parish felt the same way.

I considered leaving the parish but remembered my "Lord's Prayer" lesson and my retreat experience. I repeated the retreat forgiveness prayer ("_____ , I forgive you in Jesus' name and ask God to bless you") over and over again, calling the name of each of those who had posted or said those things. It took quite a while, but I was eventually able to find peace and once again speak to them at church. But, I must say, I'll never see them in the same way as I did before. I pray that as I seek to see Jesus in them, they may be able to see Jesus and be Jesus to *all* people, not just those who look like them.

If it is sometimes hard to forgive those I live with in the present, it is equally hard to forgive those who have harmed my people in the past. I have been fortunate to have the slave narratives of three ancestors on my mother's side. Thank God for the Catholic Church and parish records that allowed me to find the names, birthdates, baptisms and marriages of so many. Census records led me to the name of a doctor who held my great-great-grandmother in slavery—and sired her five children.

My son Curt, the priest, had a retreat experience where he was to pray for his family, starting with our nuclear family and going back generation by generation. He called afterwards and said during that exercise he saw the faces of his white ancestors, and intuited that they had raped the African women whom they enslaved. He asked if it could be true. I told him the stories that I had heard about the times of enslavement and validated his vision. He said that he knew he needed to forgive those who had been the instrument of pain and suffering, because they too were a part of him. Their blood also flowed in his veins and he needed to forgive them in order to love himself.

Again we find that God is *our* Father, not my Father or your Father. We are linked whether we like it or not. If we have been linked in the past by violence and injustice, perhaps through God's grace we can be linked in eternity by love.

The Church is made of people—good, bad, and in-between. We are called to love one another, even when we are not loved in return.

Mother Teresa said, "We should *see* Jesus in everyone we meet and *be* Jesus to everyone we meet."

Whenever I encounter fellow humans, of any faith or none, who cause me pain, I go back to the Lord's Prayer and my retreat experience—pray to find solace, peace and forgiveness. I am continually challenged to live the gospel and grow in my faith. My lifelong Catholic experiences feed my soul.

When the Shepherd Steals

Joanne Butler

A FEW YEARS AGO MY husband and I went parish-shopping. It wasn't easy. Most of them were generational—the same families attending for decades, and as newcomers we didn't seem to fit in. Then we found a small parish with a much better atmosphere. But what sealed the deal was when the head of the parish finance council stepped into the pulpit and gave the annual finance report—and the people in the pews were listening instead of sneaking out the back to the door.

A finance report might seem an odd way to renew one's faith, but it did. The message to me and my husband was: this is a church where you can place your trust, where the people in the pews matter and are invested in the life of the parish.

Trust was a big issue for us, because when we lived in the Arlington (Virginia) diocese, our former pastor had embezzled $320,000 out of our parish's weekly collection. Meanwhile, another Arlington pastor had embezzled $1.1 million. Now you can see why finding a parish with a hands-on finance council meant so much to us.

Consider this: in our former diocese, over $1.4 million dollars in donations had been stolen by two men. If they had not been priests, one or both of them would have gone to prison, but they didn't.

When I called a priest friend (in another diocese) with the news, he practically shouted into the phone: "The priest is *never* supposed to touch the money!"

I'm a cradle Catholic and my husband is a Christian (ex-Presbyterian). I was not, however, raised to be a pray-pay-obey Catholic; my mother was critical of our pastor, who drove a shiny black car while the nuns who ran the elementary school had to bum rides from parishioners. My parents were founding members of the Shrine of Saint Jude parish in Rockville, Maryland, and I'm just old enough to have faint memories of the old Latin Mass.

Later my parents moved to northern Montgomery County, Maryland, to Saint John the Baptist parish, which adopted every post-Vatican II fad with vigor. This included a priest who sermonized by playing his trumpet. My reaction was to study up on theology and to get into debates with the priest after Mass over errors in his sermon (to the distress of my mother and delight of my father).

Eventually my father had had enough of liturgical antics, and by the time I graduated from high school, we were irregular Mass attendees.

Meanwhile, my future husband was being raised in a conservative Presbyterian household. When he made his confirmation as a young teen, he was handed a box of donation envelopes as he exited the church. The message was unambiguous: as you are now a member of the "priesthood of all believers," you are responsible for contributing your time, talent, and treasure to this congregation.

My future husband and I followed the usual demographic pattern and stopped attending church as young adults.

In the early 1990s, I found a parish with a dynamic pastor, Father Franklyn McAfee, who also had a love for excellent church music. The parish was St. Lawrence the Martyr, just outside the Capital Beltway in Alexandria, Virginia. Fr. McAfee's sermons were a guide to my spiritual renewal, and later I brought my then-boyfriend along for the sermons and the music.

For Presbyterians, good preaching trumps liturgy, but good music is important too. Thus, St. Lawrence was a win-win for both of us. We married in 1996, but Fr. McAfee was transferred to another parish in 1997.

His replacement, Father William Erbacher, seemed to be as liturgically conservative as Fr. McAfee, if not more so, since one of his first acts was to move the tabernacle from a side wall to the main altar. That was wise, for whenever there's a new priest, parishioners make the inevitable comparisons—liturgical style, music, sermons, and so on.

Outwardly, Fr. Erbacher seemed satisfactory. But we parishioners could not see the crucial changes taking place behind the scenes.

At the same time, my husband had given up his federal career job and was in his first year as a doctoral student at Princeton University. Although Princeton was very generous to its graduate students, I was the primary wage earner (also employed by the federal government).

Despite our economic situation, my husband felt it was important to be sacrificial givers to the parish—a holdover from his Calvinist days. I was already registered with the parish and contributing via envelopes, but we had to do more.

As a consequence, we stuck with our 800–square-foot old row house, my battered Honda Civic, and the Buick once owned by my late mother-in-law. We ate a lot of casseroles. Fortunately, "stylish clothing" and "federal employee" are unrelated concepts, and my husband adopted the grad school uniform of jeans and flannel shirts. We took modest vacations and hung on to our home computer until its last gasp. Our one rising expense was the cost of travel between Princeton to Virginia, as my husband tried to come home as often as possible.

Imagine my shock some years later when Fr. Erbacher's successor informed me that we were one of the largest donors to the parish.

Returning to the Erbacher era, I had made a decision to become an extraordinary minister of the Eucharist. This brought me into a small community of believers and strengthened my faith enormously.

Suddenly in 2001, Fr. Erbacher disappeared. His very junior assistant took over as interim pastor. What happened?

On July 31, 2001, the *Washington Post* reported that a diocesan audit had revealed how Fr. Erbacher had deposited over

$320,000 into his personal bank account over the previous three years, mostly in cash.[1]

Remember that conversation with my priest friend? He asked about my parish's lay finance council. My reply was: "What finance council? We don't have one." He exploded again.

My diocese never told the people in the pews that each parish was supposed to have a lay finance council. Looking back, I wonder: If I had been aware that it was wrong not to have a council, what could I have done about it? Where would I have started?

As the 2001 *Post* article reported, while my diocese had rules and procedures in place for handling and depositing money, it left the responsibility for oversight to individual pastors. That's why St. Lawrence didn't have a lay finance council—Fr. Erbacher didn't want one. And his supervisor (the priest in charge of that region) wasn't checking the books either.

The diocese had set up a system that made it too tempting to steal cash.

First, many of the laity never bother to register with a parish, and simply drop cash in the collection basket. The ushers take the baskets after the collection to the sacristy, where they separate the envelopes from the cash, and put the entire collection in the church's safe (where other valuables, such as chalices, are stored).

Without a team of finance council laypeople to count the money, the large amount of cash became an attractive target. It was so easy for a pastor to open the safe (because the altar goods are stored there, he would have the combination), reach into the cash bag, and help himself to it.

I can see how it would begin: The pastor's need for a little extra money for a car repair—then money for Mom's expensive new meds—growing to include vacations, cars, and real estate. The pastor could justify his thievery by believing he deserved the cash for his hard work.

---

1. Caryle Murphy, "Probe of Priest Finds 'Financial Irregularities,'" *Washington Post*, July 31, 2001, https://www.washingtonpost.com/archive/local/2001/07/31/probe-of-priest-finds-financial-irregularities/ae844ead-0102-48ca-9e56-fc8a3d8a0cd2/?utm_term=.06c726042963.

To make matters worse, an even larger money situation erupted at the same time that the Erbacher embezzlement went public.

At nearby St. Raymond's, the pastor (Father Salvator Ciullo) had embezzled an astounding $1.1 million from that parish and another Arlington parish. According to the *Post*, in February 2002 Fr. Ciullo plea-bargained his way out of doing jail time in Fairfax County, Virginia.[2]

By the way, Fr. Erbacher appears to remain a priest in the Arlington diocese, as he was so listed in his seminary's fall 2012 magazine.[3] Our junior associate/interim pastor was transferred. The new pastor was a humble man, who took his job as the pourer of oil over troubled waters seriously.

Despite the new pastor, I remained at St. Lawrence for only a couple of years, later switching to another parish in the diocese.

My trust, however, was so damaged that just being inside a Catholic church made me feel defensive. It's that quick-walking feeling you get in a city when you've forgotten exactly where you parked your car, and suddenly find yourself on foot in a dodgy neighborhood.

Our current parish is low-church, the music's tolerable, and we use those awful disposable Oregon Catholic Press missals, but my husband and I don't care.

Our old parish, St. Lawrence, had a mix of high- and low-church services, including using so much incense my husband and I nicknamed it "Smoky Larry's."

But we learned the hard way that even if a parish has a liturgically-perfect service, good music and sermons, it doesn't inoculate a priest from evil.

2. Maria Glod, "Priest Avoids Jail in Thefts from Parishes," *Washington Post*, February 20, 2002, https://www.washingtonpost.com/archive/local/2002/02/20/priest-avoids-jail-in-thefts-from-parishes/c7fa2a1a-d572-4a7a-98bb-9e4d3d0fdf55/?utm_term=.ed6b44a69173.

3. "Congratulations Seminary Alumni," *Seminary News*, Fall 2012, 5, http://msmary.edu/seminary/alumni/seminary-newsletter/3060-SeminaryNews_fall2012_web.pdf.

Priests are fallen sinners like the rest of us. As my elementary schools nuns would have said, priests need to "avoid the near occasion of sin"—such as a large, accessible bag of cash that can be pilfered with no oversight. The diocese has a responsibility to its priests to help them avoid the sin of theft—that's why lay finance councils are so important.

Further, Fr. Erbacher's and Fr. Ciullo's embezzlements should have made Bishop Paul Loverde *extremely* angry. The undercounting of a parish's weekend "take" results in the parish underpaying its dues (a percentage of the "take") to the diocese.

I don't think it was a coincidence that the Arlington diocese had to mount a capital campaign not long after the embezzlement stories came out. In my opinion, the diocese found itself having to pay for things that could not be bought with funds from its weekly parish "dues"—because its bad-actor priests had been undercounting their parishes' substantial weekly cash intake.

The last and worst outcome of embezzlements is the loss of trust among the laity. Consider parishioners who are sacrificial givers, as they watch Father glide away in his nice car. Somehow he gets a new one every couple of years. Many parishioners, on the other hand, must struggle with their old clunkers while they fret over whether they have enough saved for the kids' college tuition and their own retirement.

Guess what happens when such a family discovers they can buy a better car if they cut their church contributions by half. (After all, shiny-car Father seems to be doing very well and can certainly get by without *our* money.)

Guess what happens when they realize that by just going to church at Christmas and Easter, they can save even more money—which they truly need in our era of stagnant wages and uncertain job futures. I'm not talking about people who covet an in-ground swimming pool; it's about those who are trying to get by and give their children a good education.

Embezzling clergy—and those whose lifestyle is very dissonant compared to the people in the pews—create an atmosphere of distrust in the parish. How can a parish build a real community of faith when there is unease about the man who's saying Mass?

What the clergy and the hierarchy often fail to understand is that the organization of the Church itself means the stakes are higher and the damage is greater when a priest betrays the trust of his congregation.

While I am not arguing for a congregational form of governance, where the laity hire and fire their clergy, I note that, unlike the Catholic Church, if a congregational church hires an embezzler, the laity have no one to blame but themselves.

In the Catholic Church, therefore, an embezzling Catholic priest causes doubt that goes far beyond his parish. It flows all the way up to the bishop. When bishops fail to take their supervisory duties seriously and allow great latitude for bad clergy behavior, they are engaging in a dangerous game—one where the stakes are growing higher as more people feel less need to attend Sunday Mass (which translates into fewer envelopes in the collection basket).

As with the clergy shortage (a disaster that was obvious decades ago) it appears some priests and bishops are willing to gamble on dubious financial behavior, at the risk of emptier pews and parish closures. If they cherish their Church at all, these men need to stop gambling with the trust of their parish.

The Scandal of Fecundity

RACHEL LAPOINTE

I GATHERED THE KIDS IN my arms, snapped up the diaper bag
and walked as quickly as I could to the car while my eyes welled
up with tears. Chris, my husband, hurried after me, asking, "What's
wrong?" but I just shook my head and walked faster.

It had happened again. The comments, the side-eye glances
and the outright dirty looks. Another Mass where I simply couldn't
pay attention to a thing, because I had to constantly try and keep
the kids from making more than a tiny peep, worried that I'd be
scolded if they weren't sitting and listening like miniature adults. It
felt to me like the old social rule of "Seen but not Heard" was the
most important thing to my fellow parishioners.

This wasn't a new walk of shame for me. This wasn't something that had happened at a church we were visiting either. This
was happening at *my* parish, my home. The parish my grandparents were married in. Where my mom and uncle had been
baptized and raised and received all their sacraments. Where my
parents were married, where they were a witness to life in the wild
1980s because the seat of honor at the wedding was taken up by
me, their oldest child, when I was a month old. It's where all but
two of my six siblings had been baptized, where we had received
most of our sacraments and had grown up. And where we had our
"section" because we often didn't take up one pew, but one and
a half, when we sat with friends and other family. Where I was
married, my sister was married, my brother was married. Where
all my children were baptized, and where I had dreams of them

making first Holy Communions and confirmations and weddings and even more and more baptisms.

In case you haven't gathered, my family is one that has embraced the Church's teachings on married life and family life. We are very visibly "open to life." I'm the oldest of seven children and we have an age span of eighteen years. My whole life I had witnessed my parents' openness to life. I came along before they were married; my mom was a senior in college and had considered aborting me (albeit for a brief moment) because that was the choice of many of her peers. She chose life and chose marriage as well. We were a very close family, partly because my mom home-schooled us for many years. We were one of the very few "large" families at our parish; everyone knew who we were. Who could miss six crazy kids at Mass every week?

With my youngest sister, my parents had to choose to be open to death. Celeste had been born with an incurable heart defect and she died at four months old, when I was only nineteen. I knew then that my parents were faithful users of Natural Family Planning (NFP). So when Celeste was born with health issues I asked myself why God would allow a pregnancy where the baby was practically born to die. It's something I still struggle with, but that openness to life and death was something that influenced my choices to stay in the Catholic faith as an adult as well as to use NFP in my marriage.

Chris and I are unconventional high school sweethearts. We started dating when I was a senior and he a junior, but we didn't attend the same school. Nor did we even live in the same state! He was 800 miles away in New Hampshire, while I was in Detroit and getting ready to go off to Ohio for college. We met on a Christian message board and bonded over love of God, Mountain Dew, and goofy videos on the internet. A year and a half long-distance, and then three years until we got married at my childhood church.

We welcomed our first child with great joy eleven months after our wedding. Not quite a honeymoon baby, but we certainly didn't wait long!

Our daughter is my "Mini Me" in so many ways. One of the biggest is that she just does not keep quiet. She was a happy baby: not colicky, but once she learned to talk, oh boy, did our energy levels have to pump to keep up with her! We knew she needed company, and our second came along twenty-three months later. The two of them have been a dynamic duo ever since and keep us on our toes.

This was when things started really getting difficult though. I was dealing with postpartum depression, and we were severely in the "underemployed" demographic, relying on government supports to keep us afloat. I wasn't flaunting the aid we received, but I wasn't shy to talk about it either.

And so the comments started. Sometimes I would just hear about some gossip from the school moms, which I'd just blow off. By this time, my youngest brothers were no longer homeschooled but attending the parish school, and I was friendly with a lot of the moms there. I looked up to a lot of them and even though I only had babies at the time I had hope that I could learn something from them and maybe have some "mom friends."

But then things started getting rougher. My kids are not low-key at all. They literally cannot sit still for more than 10 minutes. They've rarely sat still for a whole movie or TV show let alone for all of Mass.

Sitting is one issue, volume is another. "Whisper" does not seem to be in the dictionary for any of my kids until past the age of two.

So these squirrelly urchins came with us faithfully to Mass every week. It's vitally important to me that my children go to Mass and see their parents there, together, faithfully. I firmly believe that the only way children will learn to participate in the Mass is to be there, seeing it and doing it to the best of their ability. So when these little troublemakers were predictably loud and distracted, at first I was unfazed. This was normal development. Of course if they were shouting and yelling or crying profusely I'd either go to the cry room or even out of church completely, but if they were just talking to each other while coloring, or otherwise paying attention and shouting things like "Jesus! Cross! Mary!" I would do my best to keep them in the pew.

More and more, we got looks. We got comments. "Reminders" that there was a cry room, right over there behind where we sat. And so I would come into church and pretty much head right to the cry room. That cry room is smaller than most closets. It only has five chairs and two kneelers in it, along with a shelf of children's books. The only bright spot in this room were the two paintings: one a gorgeous Madonna and Child, the other a painting of my sister Celeste, whole and healed, in the arms of Jesus.

This cry room was impossible to get into some days, when it was already overtaken by other kids. And often families would just go sit in there and let their kids run wild. It wasn't a room where parents calmed their children and returned to the pew in a moment; it was like the Wild West. So if I took the kids there, they assumed it was play time with new friends.

Once an usher came up to me before Mass had even begun when one of the kids cried out. I had already calmed the baby, but he still came up and said, "You know there's a cry room over there?" "Yes, I do," I responded, "there's a picture of my dead sister in it." He walked away and I sat there with tears in my eyes, trying not to burst into tears the rest of Mass.

Another time an older lady came over after Mass and demanded to know why we brought the kids when they were so terrible, that they shouldn't come until they are old enough to behave. I cried and cried on the drive home and nearly swore to never come back. But we did, and the next week she apologized and gave the children a peace offering of cookies.

Chris, my knight in shining armor, took these things hard. He had never experienced any sort of thing like this, but of course, it was just him and one younger sister. He had never heard any sort of weird large family comments growing up, so while I tried to brush things off and minimize them, he wanted us to get out of there. And eventually the last straw came.

I'm a prolific Facebook poster. And I'm not shy about sharing things that are more private with my friends list. So one day

I shared about my frustrations with the Department of Human Services and how we were getting food benefits cut because of their error.

And the firestorm erupted.

One of my fellow parishioners, a woman whom I greatly respected for a variety of reasons, blasted us. Her criticism started out as a traditional conservative rant about food assistance programs and how no one should have kids if they need to use government assistance. It continued until she was messaging me to say things like, "You shouldn't be taking your kids to church because they are so noisy, and I'm not the only one who thinks so," and, "You shouldn't have had your kids."

When faced with this kind of thing, I'm not the type of person to just crawl into my own little hole and cry by myself. I have to do something. So for us that meant it was time to officially switch churches.

Many of my friends were raised in Protestant traditions, and I confessed to them how weird it was to be "church shopping." They all understood completely just how weird it is to go from a place where you felt secure and loved and part of a family, to having to search and test out new "families."

We knew that we could really go to any Catholic church and get the fullness of the faith. But we wanted to find a parish family that would welcome all of us, noisy children included. And we wanted it to be a place where we would be spiritually "fed," with good orthodox homilies, good music and a worship style that suited us. Thankfully we were able to find that right down the street at the next nearest parish to us.

Sometimes it's frowned upon to go to a parish that isn't your "assigned" parish. With the great abundance of Catholic churches (especially in the Northeast and Midwest, but all over the country), you are assigned to a parish based on your address. For certain sacraments, like marriage, baptism, and confirmation, you are supposed to go to your assigned parish and can sometimes need a letter from that pastor if you seek out that sacrament elsewhere. And this method is designed to help insure that parishes are supported by the people who are closest to it. But if you live in a neighborhood with a parish that ends up rejecting you, where you don't feel safe or welcome, it's not against church law to go to another parish. It might not be the norm, but it's not unheard-of or strange!

This whole trajectory of my life had me thinking about what the Church teaches regarding babies and when it is and isn't a good idea to have them. We've always used NFP for when we needed to avoid having a baby, but we also welcomed babies with open arms and hearts. All three of them were "planned," even if that planning was a moment's notice of, "Wait, why are we avoiding? There's no need for that!" and throwing it all to the wind. But now that I was being personally attacked for having any children at all when it meant relying on government aid, I had to seriously discern if we were doing God's will or being imprudent and selfish by having kids that we couldn't "afford."

Here's the thing. The Church does not teach that you have to have a certain income in order to have children. It doesn't say that you have to have $10,000 in extra income each year to solely devote to every single child (so a family of ten kids would need $100,000 just for kid expenses). It doesn't say that you need to have a savings plan in place and already saving for college expenses. The Church places *no* requirements whatsoever on what you have to have or do or be in order to have a child.

The Catholic faith teaches that we are to help the poor. We are to provide food, shelter, clothing, and moral support to those who are in a position of being unable to meet all their needs. What we are not to do, however, is to shame people. But we were being shamed for following the church's teachings on birth control. We were shamed for getting married "young" instead of living togeth-er for years to save money, or using contraception to "stay safe." And we weren't being shamed by people who didn't understand our beliefs! We were shamed by those who sat in the pews with us. We were shamed by the people who run the food bank. We were shamed by those who should be supporting us.

There's a contradiction in Catholic culture. On the one hand there are very conservative people who believe that using NFP with the intent to avoid pregnancy is exactly equal to using any form of birth control. They claim that NFP can be used with a "contraceptive mentality" where you just want to have sex for fun and avoid the consequences of a child.

But they overlook the real contraceptive mentality. The real contraceptive mentality is the one that says you should only have a baby when it's the "right time" and you have all your ducks in a row. It's the one that posts memes about welfare queens and causes a mom to feel ashamed for using her WIC benefits at the grocery store when she ends up in line next to someone she knows. The real contraceptive mentality is the one where children are shushed in church to the point that parents stop attending church. It's a church with cry rooms, but no mother support groups. It's shame and judgement and condemnation. It's the one where a couple ends up looking at each other and thinks, "Maybe we shouldn't have had our kids? Maybe we should just stop now since we're never going to get ahead financially?"

But the church can provide support without shame or judgement! We can help people get their feet under them after job loss. We can welcome children into our Masses—and smile when they do what every child does: make noise! We could offer Bible studies and classes that are at good times for families, and offer child care so that our parishioners will learn that they can have a lifelong relationship with Jesus. These things aren't against our faith; they are the things we should be doing!

I live my days right now with great hope. Since removing the stress of being on guard at every Mass I've been able to work on my relationship with Jesus. I've been able to relax and work to get the kids to learn about the Mass, while understanding that they aren't going to always be perfect. On those days where we once would have faced vocal complaints or dirty looks, instead we're told, "I've been there," or even, "I barely noticed your kids." I've learned that I'm often the most critical about the noise level and others barely even notice the kids talking quietly. We still get the occasional comment, but I've learned to brush them off, mainly because I know that our pastor believes firmly that a church full of noisy kids is a living church with a future. I've been able to work towards volunteering and actually getting involved in parish activities. I'm able to say hello to the little old lady behind me without her snapping at me about taking the kids out of church. I've become a better person and parent for it.

My spiritual journey is far from over but this has been a significant part of it. Facing criticism from those we consider to be our family is an extraordinary cross to bear. If it weren't for the graces that God has given me, we might very well have left the Church, opting for a family-friendly Protestant option. But rather, God has shown me that sometimes we need to choose our parish family based on the community that welcomes us, not the one we're assigned to by the diocese. The first step to being part of that family is to take the step of faith, to reach out and try something new and a little different. And God has led us to a parish that's truly perfect for us, one that meets all our preferences for music, liturgical style, and community. And we're excited to be part of the parish growth as we grow our family even more.

Currently, I participate in the parish leadership team and I use my experiences to remind and encourage all the parish groups to work with the young families and to be open to having them at events. I've been blessed to see that it's not a battle to get people to schedule things so that families have a chance to attend. Our parish family welcomes all families with littles and we help each other out whenever we can. I had to attend Mass without Chris and a friend sat with me to help keep an eye on the kids; she was truly an angel in that moment! I am so pleased to be part of a church family where my suggestions to make things more family-friendly are met with enthusiasm and positivity.

As I sit here now, I'm pregnant with our fourth baby. I'm ready for the challenge of raising this baby to love Jesus, to love others and to serve the Church. And I'm ready for this baby to cry in church.

To Your Grace Do I Ascribe

M. Saverio Clemente

> To your grace also do I ascribe whatever sins I did not commit, for what would I not have been capable of, I who could be enamored even of a wanton crime? . . . Is there anyone who can take stock of his own weakness and still dare to credit his chastity and innocence to his own efforts?
>
> —Augustine, *The Confessions*[1]

MORE PEOPLE SHOULD READ Augustine. And those who have read him should read him again. In recent years I've found that his work, more than that of any other thinker—with the lone exception of Paul to whom Augustine is deeply indebted—has confronted me and challenged me and forced me to reevaluate the life I've been living. Augustine has made me uncomfortable. He has offended me. And he has done so by revealing to me my own sinfulness, my own fragility, the many times I have fallen short of the glory of God.

Yet what he has not done is what many Christians do. He has not held my sin out before me while concealing his own. He has not taken the splinter from my eye while allowing the beam to remain in his (Matt 7:5). No, Augustine's great power lies in this—he confronts me not with my sins but with his own. He tells the story of a proud man, a lustful man, an angry man, a worldly

---

1. Augustine, *Confessions*, trans. Maria Boulding (New York: Vintage, 1998) 2.7.15.

man. He tells the story of himself. And yet in him, I find me. I am the "disintegrated self" he describes as being fragmented by sin. I am the one in desperate need of God's mercy and his grace.

I often find myself seeking praise for the good that I do and making excuses for the times I fall short. Upon entering grad school, this problem became all the more apparent. In the world of academia, scholars are judged by the number of publications they produce, conferences they attend, grants they receive, awards they are given;[2] one feels a constant pressure to be seen as intelligent (no, not just intelligent but more intelligent than everyone else) and one is never without the nagging worry that he is really "stupid, a fraud, always on the verge of being found out" as David Foster Wallace so rightly put it.[3]

This temptation, however, does not belong exclusively to academics. No, it is one that tempts each of us. It is present in my desire to be thanked for holding the door and my anger when I am not thanked. It is present in my compulsion to post a Facebook status about the generous tip I left my waitress and my frustration over the dismal number of likes that this status received. It is there when I struggle to admit that I am wrong and when I refuse to forgive others who have wronged me. And it is there, most of all, when I exalt myself and judge others for their sins. Augustine calls this pride. Christ calls it hypocrisy. Both condemn it. And rightly so. For, as Augustine notes, pride is the opposite of truth. When we do good, he insists, it is because we are predestined[4] to do good by the grace of God. And when we choose evil, we are really the ones who choose it. We have no one to blame but ourselves.

It is with these preliminary thoughts in mind that I would like to share some reflections on a time when a representative of

2. In short, anything that can be listed under the "accomplishments" section of their CV.

3. David Foster Wallace, "2005 Kenyon College Commencement Address," delivered at Kenyon College, Gambler, Ohio, May 21, 2005. One need only be present at the Q&A session following a paper given at a typical academic conference to know what I'm talking about.

4. His word—not mine.

my beloved Catholic Church deeply wounded someone very close to me.

My younger cousin was born out of wedlock. His father was nineteen and his mother twenty when they found out they were having a baby. They were young and unprepared and they hadn't been together very long. For those reasons and for others, it was a trying time—full of anxiety and uncertainty, decisions and doubts. Yet looking back now, it is clear to me that God was at work throughout—that he uses whatever means necessary to achieve his will.[5] Today their son, my cousin, is a sophomore in college. He is one of the kindest, most thoughtful young men I have ever known. And they, his parents, are happily married. They have been blessed with another child, a beautiful daughter, and I cannot help but admire them for all they have sacrificed and all they have given.

When he was younger, my cousin struggled with the fact that he was born to unwed parents. He never said this, of course. But it was obvious to anyone who knew him well. He was quiet, reserved, cautious when it came to trusting people. And the situation was made worse by the fact that, at times, he was judged not for the person he was but for where he had come from. He still remembers being called a "bad egg" by a friend's parent and finding out that some of his classmates were told that they weren't allowed to play with him.

Our home town of Milford is like many towns in central Massachusetts: mostly white, middle class, with a growing Latino population that brings new life and numbers to the Church community. At one point, the town was divided along cultural lines—Italian immigrants on one side, Irish on the other. Each group had its own parish, both of which are still in use, and it was not uncommon for spouses who had bridged the divide (one Italian, one Irish) to attend Mass alone rather than together so that each could remain loyal to his or her respective parish. This was the case with my mother's parents. Her father, however, died when she was a teen so my brother, cousins and I grew up attending Mass at St. Mary's of the Assumption—the predominantly Irish church.

5. Augustine really is worth reading.

As children, our Catechesis came mostly from volunteers—parents and siblings of the kids in our class—which, I assume, is the case at most parishes. Like all things, this had positive and negative consequences. On the up side, we were perhaps more likely to listen to our friends' parents than our own and certainly more than to the CCD director who, for us kids, was the very embodiment of every horror story we had ever heard about mean, old nuns.[6] As a drawback—and this became more apparent as we grew older and more inquisitive—we were often being taught by people who knew little about the faith beyond what they had learned from their volunteer CCD teachers a couple decades before. Sweeping statements like "Jesus loves you," "such and such behavior is sinful" and "sinners go to hell" become less believable and even ridiculous when given as simple answers to difficult questions. And to compound the problem, the people offering such answers often seemed less than convinced of what they were saying.

Occasionally, there would be a teacher who did take the faith very seriously and seemed to really believe what he or she taught. Yet even those instructors, in my experience, had little theological training. They often articulated their faith as one would articulate a political position—polemically, as if speaking of an ideology rather than a relationship with the living God. For these reasons and others, I spent many years away from the Church. It was only at the end of my college career when a professor and dear friend introduced me to Augustine that I began my long journey home.

But this story is not about me. It is about my cousin and how he was wounded by the Church I love. I will never forget the pain that I felt when he explained to me what had happened. He was 15 at the time and preparing to make his confirmation. He had asked me to be his sponsor only weeks before. Then, in his final weeks of CCD, his instructor chose to spend a class discussing the Church's teachings on sexuality. Unfortunately, as is often the case, the discussion revolved more around the politics of same-sex marriage

---

6. Looking back now, she really wasn't a bad woman. She had little patience for our antics, which, in her defense, were at times pretty mean-spirited.

and abortion than it did an authentic understanding of God's plan for human sexuality. It was during that discussion that my cousin was told that people who have premarital sex and conceive out of wedlock reject God's plan for his creation, that they are immoral, that they cannot provide for their children the way that other parents can, that they are sinners. He was presented with a very simplistic picture of the Church's teachings—one that lacked the nuance, care, and mercy so central to the gospel message. He was obviously very hurt and very embarrassed and so was I.

As someone who had only recently returned to the faith after years of wandering, I really struggled with this situation. First, I was hurt for my cousin. (This is perhaps how it is with every wound; the pain is not only felt by the wounded but is inflicted upon all who care for them.) But more than that, I was angry with my Church. I had been drawn back to the Catholic faith because of the Church's rich theology and because of my own need for forgiveness. Yet I now found myself feeling frustrated, annoyed, hurt, confused. I was angry that my fellow Catholics seemed to lack both the theological understanding needed to speak on difficult matters and the humility needed to do so without judgment or condemnation. I wanted to make it known that such people did not represent my Church and that they did not represent me.

That night, I went to dinner with a close friend, Father Memo, the priest who would end up marrying my wife and me. I told him about the anger I felt. I told him that I was mad at my cousin's instructor, mad at the Church.

His response surprised me. "None of us is fit to proclaim the gospel," he said. "And yet we must try."

At the time, I did not fully understand what Memo was trying to tell me. I did not realize that his words were a gentle reproach, without judgment, meant to open my eyes to my own hypocrisy and pride. But now, looking back, I recognize that the anger I felt was in many ways a perpetuation of the sin already being perpetrated. I judged my cousin's instructor for being judgmental. I condemned her for condemning others. Yet the truth is that each of us is a sinner. Each is in need of God's mercy. None is fit to proclaim the gospel. And yet, we must try. We are commanded to try (Mark 16:15).

This, I think, is the message we ought to share with those who, like my cousin, have been wounded by representatives of the body of Christ. The Church proclaims forgiveness. And she recognizes that her own members need forgiveness most of all. But forgiveness is not easy. It is not comfortable. It means recognizing our own weakness, our own frailty, our own need to be forgiven. It means recognizing that whatever sins we do not commit, those too must be ascribed to the goodness of God's grace.

"Fail of God" and Other Misadventures in Deaf Catholic Life

"Sarah"

O NE OF THE MOST enduring witnesses to Christ is the daily Mass. Wherever I am, I can locate a church, visit for a half hour, and enter the gospel story. I have found myself in chapels and oratories near and far attending to the readings, receiving Christ in the Eucharist, and pondering thoughtful homilies that provide strength for my day. Throughout my adult life, the daily Mass experience has energized my routines. I crave it. It is a daily refuge from the chill of winter, where I can rest in the warmth of the gospel.

In that space, I have been challenged to think more intentionally about the people I encounter daily. Each time I attend, I am inspired to see the incarnation. Regular attendance at daily Mass has led me to a profound appreciation of Christ's presence in the Eucharist and all the other sacraments. The reality that God nourishes us with himself so that we can nourish others would be inconceivable without the daily Mass. Had this worship experience not been readily available and accessible to me, I would not have survived the darkest periods of my life. Receiving Christ in the Eucharist each day has fueled a fire deep within my soul.

I desired to maintain my pattern of daily Mass throughout my life, and I never imagined any possible roadblock to that intention. Catholic churches are everywhere, and all people are free to seek

God therein. Every Catholic who comes has the opportunity to encounter Christ in the sacraments. How could the Mass itself be inaccessible to faithful Catholics? Until my late twenties, I found that idea preposterous. I thought the only requirement to access the Mass was to arrive with a desire to receive Christ.

I remember observing sign language interpreters at Mass from time to time when I was in graduate school. But I did not think critically about their presence and what it meant for our faith community. I had assumed that a few deaf and hard-of-hearing Catholics were part of our campus community, but I did not know any of them. I never made the effort. I had not considered that access would be a problem, particularly when an interpreter was available. My assumption was that the church could provide American Sign Language interpretation to deaf and hard-of-hearing Catholics easily and that all ASL interpreters could convey the Mass faithfully, empowering all to participate.

Then, my life changed forever, and I saw firsthand that the Mass could be out of reach for people with diverse access needs. Suddenly I began losing my hearing in the course of an illness, and I became the one using interpreter services at church. And I would have never guessed just how dreadfully wrong I had been all those years before. The daily Mass that was once a source of spiritual warmth quickly reduced to a shadow of its former self.

I had spent most of my life assuming if churches had captioning or interpreters present, then a knowledgeable person existed somewhere in the community to ensure that all access needs were being met with quality services. If the needs of deaf and hard-of-hearing Catholics were not being met, certainly the rest of the congregation would know about the issues. As Christians, we would be mobilized to ensure those needs were being met. We would hold discussions about the Americans with Disabilities Act. If nothing else, we would be speaking of our Christian duty to make the gospel accessible to everyone. If Catholics are preaching the gospel in all lands and include people of every tribe, tongue, and nation, then of course we would have adequate language provisions for access . . . right? If the Church's commitment to offering services in diverse languages was not enough to account for this, surely our commitment to serving the marginalized would be. What faithful Catholic would justify denying a deaf or hard-of-hearing person ASL-accessible worship? If the Church exists to offer a warm spiritual home to everyone, how could She leave some of Her members out in the cold?

Losing my hearing brought me face to face with these issues. Something seemed wrong to me about the idea that I just needed to take other Catholics' advice and "fix" myself. I started wearing hearing aids, but also I focused more heavily on learning American Sign Language and exploring how to enjoy living my life as my illness progressed. As others told me that the only acceptable perspective on deafness is that it is pathological and a result of the fall of humanity, my soul cried out in distress. Something about that didn't match what I was beginning to feel in the depths of my soul. The more I pondered and prayed about my hearing loss, the more evident this became.

In the process of soul-searching and seeking a place to belong, I found the Deaf[1] community; I discovered a rich, delightful culture and people who loved me, embraced me, and did not view me as broken. I never knew Deaf as a culture until its people began to adopt me as one of their own. By getting to know members of the Deaf community, I found the steady warmth of home and family. I have realized that although my experience is atypical, I need not remain alone.

The Deaf world has its own stories, norms, ways of living, and a strong sense of solidarity. It is beautiful, and I am forever enriched by encountering aspects of Deaf culture. I thank God for this discovery because it saved my life and my faith. Among Deaf Catholics, I did not need to view myself as having a deficit. The vibrant fire of faith burns bright in the hearts and souls of Deaf Catholics.

---

1. "Deaf" refers to a culture with its own history, art, storytelling, social norms, and other unique aspects. American Sign Language is a key element in American Deaf culture. This term is different from "deaf," which is a medical term referring to profound hearing loss.

As I reflected on how I experienced church differently after losing my hearing, I began to realize that hearing Catholics overlook members of the Deaf community in ways that have never occurred to them. The hearing Catholics I had known previously were unaware of any cultural differences. All simply assumed that the Church would provide for the needs of deaf and hard-of-hearing people in the congregation. I began to recall that I had not noticed many blind people, deaf people, wheelchair users, or others with different kinds of access needs in church. I had spent years thinking that people with access needs made up a tiny portion of the population. It had never dawned on me that perhaps these communities were larger, but were choosing not to attend Mass because of physical or cultural inaccessibility.

Since then I have experienced many masses where it was difficult, if not impossible, to participate fully. I desire to participate as fully as I can, yet consistently I have needed to fight for access. Although nothing physically prevents me from going to daily Mass as I had before, one barrier after another has emerged. I can access the Eucharist itself, but not other aspects of the service. If I find the readings on my iPhone to attempt following along, I risk being chided by other attendees about the disrespectfulness and distraction of cell phones at Mass. Unless an interpreter is present, I have no way to interact with the priest's homily. I can still attend daily Mass, but the experience is no longer a joy and spiritual challenge that fuels my internal fire.

That spiritual fire is fueled by worshipping in community, standing abreast with others while facing Christ. Usually, I have attended Mass a few times at a particular community before asking about access provisions. Often, parish administrators and priests have responded that everything is available in printed form in the bulletin, and that should provide all deaf and hard-of-hearing people with adequate access. Reading the prayers of the church silently does not have the same impact as joining my prayer with others in unison, which is difficult to explain to hearing Catholics who have never struggled to understand what is being proclaimed at which point in the Mass.

Proclaiming the gospel in community means joining together as one, holding space for others in our hearts and our prayers for the long term. I have inquired at Catholic parishes that have reported past attempts at offering an ASL interpreter for a deaf person, but claimed it was a distraction to the other members in the community. Unsurprisingly, eventually the deaf attendee stopped coming. Sustaining the fire of hospitality requires work.

The gospel has its own unique language conveying theological truths to the faithful. Fanning the flames of the gospel means that everyone proclaiming the gospel at Mass can communicate core theological concepts. I have attended Masses where the interpreter is highly skilled, yet lacks theological knowledge about Catholicism. Countless times I have watched interpreters sign "the communion of saints" using the sign used for the Eucharist, thus conveying "the Eucharist of saints" instead of the community of the faithful past and present. Although usually I can figure out the intended meaning, it interrupts my ability to enter fully into the message. But in these circumstances, a deaf or hard-of-hearing child without much catechesis experience might grow up missing important theological concepts.

If skilled and trained interpreters can make errors that impact how deaf and hard-of-hearing people receive the gospel, these problems only increase when churches rely on volunteer interpreters with unknown signing skill levels. The catechetical function of the Mass suffers when the interpreter's skills are underdeveloped. Deaf and hard-of-hearing Catholics might attend Mass only to see the interpreter sign, "*Fail* of God, you take away the sins of the world," or that "the *guilt* of God" is the core concept of a homily devoted to "the *grace* of God." Those who do not know ASL would never realize these malapropisms exist. A parish should not be faulted for relying on volunteer interpreters when money is tight. Nonetheless, it has been disheartening to see people who have no knowledge of American Sign Language congratulate the interpreter for "beautiful interpretation" or thank the interpreter for adding to their worship experience when the deaf and hard-of-hearing Catholics using the interpreter have been confused throughout the entire liturgy. Many hearing Catholics do not even think about asking deaf and hard-of-hearing congregants about how they have experienced the Mass. Consulting with deaf and hard-of-hearing people about the quality of access and how it could be improved given the parish's resources is crucial.

Experiencing Mass fully adds fuel to our individual spiritual fires. Entering into a community's ministerial life sustains the flame. We receive the Eucharist in order to offer Christ to the world. Yet rarely do hearing Catholics dream about ministering with deaf and hard-of-hearing Catholics. Most hearing Catholics would not think to ask deaf Catholics about interest in homeless ministry or serving as lay liturgical ministers. Too often, Catholics view deaf and hard-of-hearing ministries as benevolence rather than inclusion of cultural diversity. Access concerns become a checklist where hearing people focus on the logistics of checking the boxes. Benevolence ministries rarely ask questions about full participation in every facet of the community's life. When the focus is on printing bulletins and finding ASL interpreters, little time remains for reflecting on how deaf and hard-of-hearing people contribute their gifts to the broader parish community. Deaf people already serve in every ministerial capacity within Deaf parishes, including the priesthood. How might the lived experience of church be different if every ministry were designed with the goal of welcoming the gifts and talents of its core constituents? Outsiders with a passion for serving others might *initiate* a ministry; yet, ministries *thrive* when they are guided and directed by their core constituents.

Deaf Catholic culture, while just as faithful as hearing Catholic culture, is distinct. Whether deaf and hard-of-hearing Catholics attend a Deaf parish or participate in a majority hearing parish, we have many gifts to offer the Church. The body of Christ is made stronger when all the Church's members are cared for and participate fully. Deaf and hard-of-hearing Catholics challenge all Catholics to rethink how ability has been traditionally perceived and interpreted in scripture. A common view defines deafness as an affliction, so hearing Catholics may be surprised to learn that culturally Deaf people do not wish to become hearing. Interacting with people from diverse cultural traditions allows everyone to catch a glimpse of what it means to be a Church of every tribe, tongue, and nation. Understanding how people of different hearing statuses encounter Christ would mean more opportunity to reflect deeply on the miracle stories of the gospel, what it means to listen to God, and how God reveals himself to his people.

I long for a warm spiritual home where I can stoke my own spiritual fire. I attend services regularly, but I feel like I am invisible even though I'm sitting in the front row. Remaining in the church is a challenge. Although my local area has significantly more deaf and hard of hearing access than one would find in most communities across America, I grieve the loss of full participation within my parish. My hope for the possibility of more meaningful deaf and hard-of-hearing ministry sustains me.

I have seen how resilient Deaf culture is, and I know other deaf and hard-of-hearing Catholics committed to remaining Catholic. I have seen an insatiable hunger for the sacraments and passion for the gospel. I will always remember how hordes of deaf and hard-of-hearing Catholics arrived for Mass when a visiting Deaf priest presided in ASL. The resilience and solidarity of this community sustains and empowers no matter how many times I encounter hearing people with misconceptions about what it means to be Deaf. Come what may, I believe with all my heart that the Eucharist not only strengthens us individually but also binds us together into one body who cares for all its members. I have seen deaf and hard-of-hearing Catholics faithfully ministering to one another even when no one else will. We remain fiercely loyal to each other, to the Catholic Church, and to God no matter how high the odds get stacked against us.

Part III: Reclaiming the Faith

This final part is focused on hard questions of personal spirituality.

Jason E. Gillikin describes moving past resentment after he was rejected by a seminary and had to completely reimagine how his life would unfold. He begins with a moment of startling spiritual clarity—it even takes place in a garden!—but his decision to pursue ordination, inspired by that clarity, was ultimately thwarted. What do you do when your *only* mystical experience seems to have led you into failure? Gillikin explores the answers he has found.

Catherine Addington contributes a meditation on the way women saints' images have been misused. She looks at all of the "saints Catherine," all of her namesake saints, and finds in each one of them an unexpected resonance with her own experience in the Church.

Gabriel Blanchard, who blogs at Mudblood Catholic, contributes a passionate poem, packed with liturgical and sacrificial imagery, from the perspective of a gay Catholic experiencing a crisis of faith. This is a poem without an easy resolution. Our fidelity to the Church will often look like sacrifice on an altar. Blanchard's honesty makes the poem's final image of grace all the more powerful.

A Moment of Clarity

JASON E. GILLIKIN

I WAS BLESSED WITH THE only truly mystical religious experience of my life just after noon on Good Friday, on a glorious spring day in 2000, as I prayed the rosary in the garden at the Legion of Christ novitiate in Cheshire, Connecticut. The memory remains, perfect, unsullied: I sat on a bench, near a statue of the Blessed Virgin, and for a few moments, I enjoyed the gift of profound clarity. Everything made sense. *Everything*.

The moment passed, and the clarity eventually faded, but the experience still serves as a spiritual anchor, securing me to a personal mission of ministry to the people of God. And although I didn't realize it at the time, that brief communion with the Divine also infused me with the grace I needed to survive the near occasion of sin—that is, formation for the priesthood—without resenting God or the Church.

Some history: I sat in that garden that day because I was gently goaded by a priest—one of the Franciscan friars in residence at my home parish in West Michigan—to explore the religious life. I had already declared my intent and proceeded through the necessary screens and paperwork to enroll in the diocesan vocation program. The friar wanted me to be a Franciscan, although he never said so directly; instead of visiting a Franciscan retreat house, however, I spent Holy Week with the LCs.

The Legion's charism drew me, on paper, but through that visit I discovered the order to be an imperfect fit. It didn't dawn on me until I was deep into the process that by going to Cheshire in the first place, I had probably doomed my priestly aspirations from the start.

Several years after my relationship with the vocations program ended, after my pursuit of ordained ministry collapsed, I heard from a high-ranking diocesan official that the Most Rev. Walter Hurley, the then-new bishop of Grand Rapids, was "looking into" the priestly formation program and that my file, among others, was under review. Before Bishop Hurley's arrival, the program was perhaps more of an afterthought than it should have been. The long-time vocations director was a good man, and a faithful priest, but from seminarians and newly ordained alike, I had heard one consistent message: "Smile and nod, study hard, toe the party line—and after you're ordained, you can finally be authentic."

As with many other diocesan vocation programs over the last few decades, the guardians of ordination in my diocese tended to be what one wag called the "bitter clingers of *aggiornamento*." In other words, the vocation offices were often staffed with clergy or lay ministers who placed a premium on pastoral concerns, including liturgical flexibility, while downplaying strict liturgical fidelity and the less-convenient parts of the Magisterium. If an aspirant were deemed to be too "rigid" (code for "conservative") then extra hurdles tended to pop up. By going to Cheshire, I had raised all the relevant red flags, and it wasn't until a *third* set of interviews that a kindly priest said, "You know, the LCs have a reputation that the vocations office doesn't care for."

I completed all those extra interviews and spiritual-direction sessions, each one successfully, only to be rejected at the very end by the rector of the one seminary I was allowed to apply to, for reasons as inconsistent as they were vague. Years of engagement, a degree in philosophy, time spent volunteering, a semester in residence—all of it apparently for naught.

The ultimate slap in the face? I called the vocations director after I received my rejection letter. When I asked what we'd do next he said, "Well, you need to think of something else to do with your life."

That comment stung.

And it's not just the resentment, the pain, the *humiliation* of having been casually disregarded by the seminary. Those emotions—and I felt them intensely!—weren't just mine, because I didn't walk the journey alone. My face still blushes when I remember having to explain to fellow parishioners, lifelong friends and neighbors who cheered me on, why the process ground to a halt. I remember the disappointment in my grandparents' face when their dream of having "their family priest" was taken away from them. And I remain grateful, in a humbled sort of way, that my parish's deacon—with whom I sometimes disagreed on liturgical matters—drew me closer, to the point of advocating for me as a lay volunteer with the diocesan worship office.

Of course, all that goodwill notwithstanding, there's nothing quite as disconcerting as having a member of the Little Old Ladies' brigade at 7:30 a.m. Mass whisper, at 240 decibels, "Wasn't he supposed to be a priest? What happened? Wasn't he good enough? Such a shame."

I admit: at first, I was angry. Hurt. Disappointed. I did everything asked of me. I gave years of my life to pre-seminary formation. I spent a big chunk of my twenties living a godly life instead of invoking Augustine's maxim of being holy "but not yet."

Did I resent rejection? Of course. After all, I had that moment of clarity a few years prior. I thought I had the answer. I thought I had a *vocation*—God told me himself, on Good Friday, no less. To be derailed because I wasn't liberal enough? What an outrage!

And I wanted "justice." I wanted the vocations director to be put out to pasture. I wanted some outward sign to which I could point my supporters, saying, "It's not that I wasn't worthy, it's that they weren't worthy of me."

For a few months, still numb and somewhat in denial, I went through the paces, as if on autopilot. I still did my pastoral-care visits in the hospital and in prison. I still volunteered as a sacristan and lector and extraordinary minister of the Eucharist at Mass.

It was this habit of ministry, emotionally empty though it was at the time, that brought me face to face with one very special hospital patient, several months after I received my rejection letter.

I don't remember his name. What I *do* remember is that the fellow was a World War II veteran who outlived his wife and children. He had been admitted for something not very serious, and he was on my visit list because he had identified as Catholic. When I visited, I offered him Communion, which he accepted, but what he really wanted was my time. So I gave it to him. More than an hour, as I recall. He was a delight, telling me stories of the war and of his family and of his job as a sales executive.

It was a great visit. After I left, it hit me, hard, that all the man wanted was someone to talk to. It was just that simple. And I ministered to him. I didn't even need a collar or a cassock. In recognizing the power of that simple ministry, I confronted a truth that, I suppose, I had willfully ignored—that my personal mission, settled in Cheshire, had been based on my own assumptions about what ministry entailed. It had never occurred to me to inquire of God what such ministry ought to look like until he smashed the artifice of my ambition.

It was embarrassing—no, *humiliating*—to be rejected by the seminary. But such pain was a very small price to pay for that gift of blessed clarity in a peaceful garden on a warm spring day, and the lasting kernel of faith and of ministry that blossomed from it.

I'm no longer on the path to priesthood, but because of that experience—starting in Cheshire, ending in a hospital room—I take comfort in believing that I'm a better servant because of it.

A Name Which No One Knows

Catherine Addington

To the victor I shall give some of the hidden manna;

I shall also give a white amulet upon which is inscribed
a new name,

which no one knows except the one who receives it.

—Revelation 2:17

I N THE CATHOLIC CHURCH, a name is more than style. A name
is given in baptism as a point of entry into tradition, uniting
a child with the communion of saints. The act recalls the biblical
renaming of the apostles: you have been called for a purpose, a
mission, that is holiness. And with these syllables we will remind
you of that every time we identify you, in conversation, in scold-
ing, in prayer. Traditionally, a child is given a saint's name, so that
with the name comes the gift of a patron—a spiritual companion,
an example, and an intercessor in heaven as they embark on their
journey in the faith.

My patron was, technically, ambiguous. There are a great
many saints Catherine, just as there were countless Catherines
in my Catholic school. We all wore uniforms: us, plaid jumpers;
them, habits and scars. It was an odd sisterhood, one I spent a lot
of time with. While distracted throughout twice-weekly Mass, I'd
imagine my heavenly posse. I'd see Caterina de' Ricci, the old prioress, trading tales of Italian convent life with Caterina da Genova
and Caterina Volpicelli, while Kateri Tekakwitha and Katharine

Drexel gave our American grin. Catherine Labouré's Marian poetry gave Caterina da Bologna inspiration for painting. Katarina av Vadstena tagged alongside her old friend, Caterina da Siena, who undoubtedly had important business to discuss. Catherine of Alexandria, for her part, was distantly regnant in that golden-mosaic way of early martyrs. I was more imaginative than pious, more distracted than devout. But underneath my reverie was a distinct sense of belonging. There was glory ahead. This had been done before. I'd never have to go it alone.

🐜 🐜 🐜

My sixth-grade classroom was tiny and crowded, an uncomfortable place to have important conversations. When the parish priest visited, whether to help with religion class or—as on this particular day—on business, he rarely knew what to do with the acoustics. His preaching was always rendered a bit awkwardly loud. On that day, we had learned the bishop had given permission for girls to serve at the altar, a first for our diocese. The priest was visiting to inform us that our parish would not be taking part in this new policy. I was front row and furious—a posture I got used to—and, to no one's surprise, the first to raise my hand.

I looked around, made a class headcount (seven boys, twenty girls), and rolled my eyes. "How come the nuns who teach here get to be altar girls in their chapel, but we don't get to be in our chapel?"

I don't remember what he answered. I doubt I was listening. All I remember is that same priest chatting with my mother when she came to pick me up after school. "You definitely named her after the right woman." We knew the one he meant: Caterina da Siena, or as I called her then, the woman who told the pope where to go.

As a teenager that's exactly how I thought of her, that Renaissance woman, demanding that the pope return from Avignon, serving as an ambassador in times of turmoil, preaching like some kind of holy fool. I admired her loudness, I think, more than anything. I was in love with my faith in that age's infatuated way, going to Mass every day, leading a youth group, trying to take over religion class. It was the perfect forum for adolescent intensity. What were people going to say? *Hey, chill with the church thing?* So I wore Caterina's name like a badge of honor. *If you are who you ought to be, you will set the whole world on fire,* she is so often quoted.[1] I copied it in my notebook. This is what women do in our church, I announced to others and convinced myself, they speak truth to power and demand unpopular holiness.

It was a protective self-image. No matter how many things irritated me about the Catholic Church, I could not only stay in the Church, but revel in my rabble-rousing part in it. Caterina da Siena was my shield from the uncertainty on the other side of my self-righteousness.

I held on to her tight.

❧ ❧ ❧

Caterina de' Ricci suffered the Passion every week for twelve years. Her suffering was consistent, scheduled even, but it felt random, the way each in a predetermined set of scourges feels fresher and fiercer and endless. Many pilgrims—spectators—visited her monastery to see her, to pray, to watch her writhe and bleed. Her sisters had no peace. They had to care for these pilgrims who flooded their home, and for Caterina, who as prioress was meant to be their mother. She had always confused them, frightened them in a way. As a novice, she was always dropping food, falling suddenly asleep, breaking plates, stopping midsentence. They grew to understand these things as side effects of mystical ecstasy, but they bore them all the same as volatility, the sort of chaos they thought they left outside the convent walls. Even so, she was a gift to them, a caring and wise woman who advised popes and saw God.

Imagine being one of Caterina's sisters. Imagine the pilgrims bleeding through the front door, hungry, needy, and noisy. Or,

---

1. Original quote: "If you are what you ought to be, you will set fire to all Italy, and not only yonder." Catherine of Siena to Stefano Marconi, in Vida D. Scudder, trans. and ed., *Saint Catherine of Siena as Seen in Her Letters* (New York: Dutton, 1906) 305.

worse, fancy, courtly, and out of place. Being hospitable means breaking the fast. You never know whether you are doing the right thing. This woman whom you love, who fights for you, who prays for you, who you have to believe suffers for you, it is so hard not to resent her. She is in pain and her pain is a nuisance and she cannot wall off the world for you even though that is her job. She is a saint, you know this, you live with a saint and she is a pest, and what does that make you? This bleeding is what it is to be holy, everyone says so, the crowds say so, and you are nothing like it. You grow old with her, this blood in your eyes, until you get together and beg God to stop, please, we need peace, we came here for peace. And he listens to you. Because you asked, she stops bleeding. The crowds stanch at long last. And now you wonder why you didn't ask twelve years earlier. Caterina's wounds might never heal, and you have to live with that, and with God being closer than you bargained for.

I know I should read that as gift accepted, sacrifice made, need met. But when I consider Caterina and her sisters, they frighten me with their female mysticism, so hideously literal. Not that women have a monopoly on stigmata, let alone on suffering. It might be better to call it a pattern, a penchant. I thought of Caterina's sisters when I was in eighth grade, looking for a confirmation saint and finding them all with open wounds. They were cloistered, festering mystics, or else virgins sacrificed to imperial greed. They were saints, I knew that, they were saints and I was frightened of them and what did that make me? I felt so guilty, standing in a crowd of pilgrims flocking to these bleeding women, trying to play along, trying to see God in them, and not being able to. I was quietly resentful, scared, confused, the way I imagine Caterina's sisters were, but like them, I was not willing to put my trust and obedience to my tradition aside. So I did the usual thing and picked the prettiest name I found: Lucia, martyred under Diocletian in the year 304. It was comforting to me that the rest of her story—eyes gouged, fire resisted, wonders done—was almost definitely mere legend.

I thought characterizing the stories that worried me as legend, as historical, as distant, would keep them from doing much damage. I didn't think of Caterina da Siena's self-starvation when

I took Lenten fasting too seriously, when I found myself cold all the time, when I chalked up my headaches to eye strain instead of my obvious hunger pangs. I didn't think of Caterina de' Ricci's holy wounds when I unconsciously channeled my anxieties into picking at my skin and the insides of my cheeks. I thought of them later, when I was working on healing myself, and praying for the strength to overcome these things. I looked up and everything I wanted freedom from was wearing a halo. I found myself among the sisters again, guilty for not seeing God in any of this.

I forgot the end of Caterina de Ricci's story, where her sisters admit their fear, their exhaustion, their longing for peace. I forgot to ask for another way.

🐝 🐝 🐝

Caterina Volpicelli loved the world. She surrounded herself with music, art, literature, theatre, dance, the things of high society. What she got in school wasn't enough for her. She made it her life, and then God crept in. Her call to religious life was sudden, rapid, urgent, the way everything is when you're a teenager. A Franciscan she met, the later Saint Ludovico da Casoria, spotted this gleeful devotee and encouraged her to pursue her goal of service to God. Stay in this society you love so much, he said to her. Become a fisher of souls. Make it all the more worthy of your love.

Caterina wanted to do him one better, to give everything she had. She entered a monastery of the Perpetual Adorers of the Blessed Sacrament, swept up in the romance of it all. What better literature than Scripture, what better theatre than liturgy, what better music than her sisters chanting?

It made sense, until it didn't. Her health forced her to leave the monastery, and she wondered what she could have possibly done wrong. God asked for her life, and she gave it to him with gusto. Why didn't he accept her sacrifice? Why was she cast back out into the world, the one she so willingly gave up for him?

I too grew up in a home full of history books and piano music, and what I got in school was only the beginning for me. My curiosity was my life, and then God crept in. He'd always been there, really; I had a religious family and a religious school. When I was confirmed and headed off to high school, it changed between us. I felt the formative part of my life was past me, and now it was time for action. I was a teenager. I was a hundred miles an hour. I was not interested in waiting for anything.

I fell in with a religious order that turned out to be manipulative and cruel, and though the trial wore religious dressing, it was no different from any experience of being young, trusting, and outnumbered. I was made to think the concerns of my family were the work of the devil, that my occasional hesitation in discernment was mere temptation, that misgivings existed to be overcome rather than to warn. The things I love most about myself—enthusiasm, imagination, optimism—became tools of abuse.

With the help of family, friends, and counselors, I got names for the things that had happened to me. I hadn't known abuse could be anything but physical. The version of me that emerged from this experience had symptoms I couldn't point at and apply medicine to. I felt overpowering trepidation when I approached confession, because of how much guilt I'd been trained to feel. I felt a defensive instinct to secrecy whenever family or friends wanted to check in with me, because my trust had been completely displaced and made me insecure. I had an intense flight response when I walked into a church, because subconsciously, for years, I'd been made to think my salvation was dependent on a group I was no longer part of—and I didn't know how to relate to God outside of that. These weren't things I could even articulate at the time, let alone know how to fix.

The only thing I never got a word for was that feeling Caterina had before me: feeling that God had asked for your life, and then spat it back out at you. How awful to feel deceived by God.

It turned out that Caterina was called to something that didn't exist yet. Her vocation came into being with her country: as wars of unification raged, cholera spread, sewage stank in the streets, and misery reigned. Ludovico's words rebounded. Caterina became a missionary to her own people. Her order opened orphanages, started libraries, fostered a youth organization, built a shrine, dedicated themselves to adoration and reparation, prayed for religious freedom and a place in the city of God. And then she did the worst thing a foundress can do: she died young, leaving a swarm of desperate novices, a suffering city, and a new nation behind her. Her sense of timing, as always, was off.

As was mine. But I wonder how Caterina's life would have been if Ludovico's words had sunk in a bit sooner, if the idea that she was called to something that didn't exist yet had been comfortable. To think that in thousands of years the Church has not yet had your genius is both headstrong and obviously true, in the way the gospel is. She helped me dare to think that, to say, perhaps sainthood is just finding new names for old things. Perhaps God spat us out for being raw, unprepared.

❧ ❧ ❧

When Tekakwitha was ten, her village was burned. Nations warred all around her, and she and her friends were employed to feed the fighters and bury the dead. Cosmologies fought, too, and families. Violence was common but never quotidian.

Tekakwitha was named for her near-blindness, the way she felt her path with her hands. Smallpox had scarred her face and impaired her eyes. The rest of her scars would be self-inflicted.

When she and her friends, all young Native women and converts to Christianity, heard that the Jesuits flagellated themselves in private, they wanted to be a part of it. It felt secret, and serious, and sacrificial. Kateri, as she was then called in baptism, excelled at this exotic penance. She had always been sick, but now her sufferings were mystical. Her world had always been violent, but now it was for a purpose. These forces that defined her life were within her control. They had narrative. They had significance.

I know what it is to crave that control. With the order that abused me, control was everything. Not just their control over me, but my control over my destiny. With an abuser, you are made to feel indispensable, to feel that your every action has enormous consequences, so that you can avoid the punishment that comes with imperfection. It is a recipe for incredible self-awareness, because

89

every small decision is high-impact. I later understood that it was classic psychology: make the victim strive for perfection, and then make them depend on you to reach it. Christ has no place in that system. Nor does your own littleness.

So I can never resent Kateri for the actions that so scared me in other saints, their self-flagellation, the burning coals at their feet. I know how she felt, despite vastly different circumstances. It is incredibly addictive to feel like the central agent in your own salvation.

Kateri is known as patron of ecology and the environment. Why? You know why. But I choose instead to think of her as the patron of survivors of war, the women and the children, shuffled around from family to makeshift family. And the patron of best friends, like her and Marie-Thérèse, the Oneida woman whose arms she died in. Most of all, the patron of radical adolescent girls, the ones who find weird and wonderfully specific communities, who think of themselves as up against the world, embarking on greatness together. The ones like her, and like me.

And I think of her as the patron of the scars on my arms, and in my cheeks, and on my shoulder blades, the ones my anxiety wore into me over the years around the order, the ones I haven't managed to stop quarrying even now. Kateri had the gospel to write her injuries into. I have her.

⁂ ⁂ ⁂

Caterina da Bologna was a child at the Duke of Ferrara's court, educated, artistic, built for success no matter what she chose. It's hard to know if she became a nun to escape that world or to further indulge in it, if her paintings survive as relics of her sanctity or her talent. It is mostly hard to imagine her caring. She spent her life as a Poor Clare, eventually and reluctantly becoming an abbess, a caring soul, a humble preacher, a quiet painter of rosy-cheeked saints and illuminated manuscripts. There was a kind of softness about her, the superior who thought herself inferior, who preferred the silence of the studio and the chapel to the buzz of aristocracy.

And yet she lived the austere, haystack life of a Franciscan and left behind writings that document visions of God and Satan alike, including her famous treatise on spiritual warfare. She listed seven weapons in the fight against evil: diligence in doing good; recognition that good cannot be done alone; trust in God; meditation on the life, passion, and death of Jesus; remembering mortality; focusing on heaven; and cherishing sacred scripture. Hearing her speak of them as weapons is as jarring as hearing her talk about weapons at all. There is something so dress-up about it all, this voluntarily barefoot noble artist, this gentle soul cautioning of the devil around every corner.

She was so normal, so aggressively normal, so full of life and art and talent. She was so young, so occupied with worldly things, always producing, always creating. Where was she hiding this faith of hers? Is she serious? Am I supposed to just take her word for it? How could she be so stalked by fear? Wasn't she doing just fine?

The first boy I told about my past laughed. There was something so dress-up about it all.

⁊ ⁊ ⁊

Catherine Labouré spent most of her life caring for the sick and elderly alongside other Daughters of Charity. But she chose that order because of a dream she had about its founder, St. Vincent de Paul. It was those dreams that would make her name. Those dreams where Mary warned her of the evil times she lived in—she was not wrong, the Church was suffering in the age of Napoleons and rebellions and uncertainty—and gave her a mission. Or rather, an image, which became the Miraculous Medal: twelve stars, two pierced hearts, and the name of Mary on one side, and the open-handed Blessed Mother, with rays coming from her hands, on the other. The prayer around her read, "O Mary, conceived without sin, pray for us who have recourse to thee."

One detail stood out. Some of the rays of light from Mary's hands did not arrive to land. Catherine asked why. (Mary said that they are the graces for which people forget to ask.) I cannot overstate the importance of this: Catherine asked why.

I asked church authorities why they let the order continue with their manipulative behavior. I asked myself why I was so foolish. I asked God why he let me go through it all, why the rays of healing and perspective and understanding that everyone around me seemed to have never reached me, why I was so angry and hurt all the time, why what I was doing to fix things wasn't enough.

I waited.

After a few years, I understood that when your spiritual life becomes about guilt and control, dependent on the wrong source of salvation, you forget to ask for grace. You think you have to earn it.

Catherine's is the name I raise in victory every time I go to confession, get honest with God, admit I got lost. Those were the graces for which I forgot to ask, for which I had forgotten I was allowed to ask. They are the graces that brought me back when my anger and sadness had driven me out of the Church. And they are exactly that: graces.

🙜 🙜 🙜

Baron von Hügel wants to know why Caterina da Genova never referred to God as father, friend, or bridegroom. It is unthinkable, to him, in writing a book on her spirituality, that she would have omitted such titles. It is "abstract," he says, "impersonal," that Caterina should deal directly with God, forsaking relational conduits, ridding herself of metaphors. They are, for her, a waste of time. "This comes no doubt, in part, from the circumstance that she had never known the joys of maternity, and had never, for one moment, experienced the soul-entrancing power of full conjugal union," he concludes. "It comes, perhaps, even more, from her somewhat abnormal temperament, the (in some respects) exclusive mentality which we have already noted."[2]

Abnormal, then. Let her be called abnormal. It is not for the Baron's eyes, this need of Caterina's to go directly to the source.

2. Friedrich von Hügel, *The Mystical Element of Religion as Studied in Saint Catherine of Genoa and Her Friends* (London: J. M. Dent, 1908) 229.

God the father, God the friend, God the bridegroom, what a waste of syllables. God contains it all. It is less than a breath to say his name, unadulterated by all those titles. Why associate God with fatherhood, a distant vocation as far as she knew? Or friendship, when his companionship was so obvious? Or marriage, when hers was a torment she prayed to escape? No, better to be direct. God knew his worth. She didn't have to state it for him.

When Caterina realized God's love for her one March day, she left without even finishing her confession. She didn't need to hear the priest say absolution. She knew. She never prayed the rosary again. *The Lord is with thee.* It wasn't necessary. She knew. She didn't wait until Sunday for communion. She went every day. She didn't wait for her husband to take his faith seriously. She took it seriously enough for both of them, working at a hospital day and night. Once her husband had squandered away all his other options, he caught up with her and came to work and pray beside her. They moved into the hospital. She ran it. And all the while, visions and ecstasies and tremors, until she could not tell the difference between heaven and earth.

Abnormal indeed. Caterina did not call God father, friend, bridegroom. She called him "I." She wrote: "My I is God, nor is any other self known to me except my God."[3] He was not distant enough to need analogy. She got so lost, so lost in God.

I knew my abnormality, that feverish passion in my faith, that dress-up radicalism could be a weapon. Caterina reminded me it can be a saving grace, to get lost in the right thing.

❦ ❦ ❦

Katharine Drexel asked the pope to send missionaries to her bleeding America and he said *why not you?*

She shrugged, went home, and got to work.

God gave Katharine an incredibly turbulent century of life, and at every turn she responded with extraordinary grace. She

---

3. *Life and Doctrine of Saint Catherine of Genoa,* trans. Connelly (New York: Christian Press Association Publishing Co., 1907) 21.

was a white woman who saw the emancipation of slaves, the rise and fall of "separate but equal," and the birth of the civil rights movement, and decided to give her life in the service of African-Americans. She was a millionaire heiress who had the Great Depression to inform her of the reality of poverty, and gave up her fortune to become a nun anyway. She was an Easterner for whom the displaced and massacred Native Americans she read about were not the distant defeated, but her urgent concern, and cause to leave the comfort of her home to act. She saw two world wars, two Red scares, and two atomic bombs, and kept her eyes trained on spiritual warfare. She gave away her money, her life, and her reputation in service of God and neighbor. Katharine Drexel was, by all accounts, a phenomenal human being.

Yet for all of Katharine's achievements—fifty missions for Native Americans, a system of black Catholic schools in thirteen states, and the first black Catholic university in the United States—what ultimately impresses me the most was that initial moment of decision. She saw a need, asked for a solution, and realized she was the providence she sought. This takes such an odd, unexpected humility, to see yourself as part of the thing people pray for when they beg God for help. She did not think of vocation as some secret plan of God's that would be explained in due time, but as something made evident by her circumstances, a decision to put her gifts at the service of God and his suffering ones.

Katharine did not see her resources as her own. She saw herself as their steward, not their owner, and understood herself as a conduit for God's providence. This could easily have been interpreted as a call to distant charity, but she understood not just her money, but also her time, energy, and passion as resources to be given in harmony—and in full. She was fantastically single-minded that way.

I have tried to learn from that ability of Katharine's to see resources for others in herself. I have stopped trying to sew up my past, to provide it with a neat ending. I have started to think of it as something to live with, rather than something to get over; as something to invite people into, an occasion for emotional hospitality. I have started to think of my pain as a resource, an opportunity for communion with others who have suffered. It is odd, at first, to think of a cross as a gift, but it is the Christian mindset at its most fundamental. It is much stranger to think of your own cross that way. What could God possibly want with this, with me? Well, *why not you?*

§a §a §a

I no longer use my patronesses as shields from my own doubts, the way I used to when I was a little girl. It's impossible to hide behind them now, when they are the ones who remind me of those doubts, who push me further into them, in order to come out stronger on the other side.

While I was in college, far from home, trying to make a new life for myself, I was received into the Orthodox Church. I felt welcomed there, among kind and gentle people who were willing to wrestle with God alongside me. It was a practical choice, too. The Orthodox tradition is theologically and liturgically distinct enough from Catholicism to allow those bruised by the latter to form new relationships with God without triggering bad memories. At the same time, the two Churches share enough history and substance to feel reasonable to one another. I encountered many differences between the two traditions, but the most unexpected and ultimately fruitful one was a mere bit of trivia: of the patronesses I'd been given at my Catholic baptism, only one of them was reverenced in the Orthodox Church as well. And that lone ecumenical Saint Catherine was the one I used to avoid the most.

Despite sharing her name, despite also being from a city called Alexandria, despite being a young woman like her who dreamed about the kingdom of God, I wrote off Catherine of Alexandria early on. I figured her just another cookie-cutter legend from the early Roman days. After all, that's all I knew her as—"Glorious Saint Catherine, virgin and martyr"—and I rolled my eyes at her. Real women do not go by "virgin and martyr." There is no nuance, no personhood in that. She could have nothing to teach me.

My Orthodox confessor felt very strongly otherwise. He and his wife believed Catherine of Alexandria had something to teach all of us, so much so that they named their daughter after her. They announced this fact proudly upon meeting me, before introducing me around the parish, particularly to other people my age. It was the first of many small actions that made me feel safe and welcome in their church, even as the most foreign of visitors. My confessor came to be a real source of guidance, support, and protection for me as I navigated learning to be vulnerable in a church again. When people in the parish sought to take advantage of me, he stood up for me, time after time.

Catherine of Alexandria finally intervened after one particularly taxing episode of church melodrama. (There is no untheatrical way to describe it: that time my seminarian boyfriend turned out to have a fiancée, but lied to me about it in the hopes that I would be gone by the time her green card came through.) After finding out and dealing with what needed to be dealt with, my confessor took me aside and recounted the story of his daughter's naming. "We named her this because we wanted her to know what glory God is capable of in his saints." He nodded encouragingly, as if to say, as he often did to me, *you have a bright future too.* "Pray to your patron saint, the great martyr Catherine of Alexandria, tonight."

When it settled in that I'd been used and manipulated by a church official—if you could call my ex that—again, the last thing I wanted to do was pray, let alone to this cartoon of a patron saint. But after everything my confessor had done for me, I was willing to indulge him a bit, so I did.

Upon revisiting Catherine of Alexandria's story, I saw that I had been unjust to her. She was a virgin and a martyr, yes, but she was first and foremost a defiant preacher, a philosopher, a teacher. The title of virgin puts the emphasis on what she kept out, but the much stronger witness is what she allowed in. This is a woman who engaged with the world, a woman to whom the Roman emperor sent philosopher after philosopher in hopes of converting her to paganism, philosophers she welcomed, philosophers she convinced. This is a woman who warmly received the servants of the state that persecuted her as fellow Christians, who prayed without ceasing, at home, in prison, before the court.

The title of martyr puts the emphasis on what was done to her, when the emperor had her tortured and killed, but the much stronger witness is what she did. This is a woman who let her cross be crafted elsewhere rather than ambitiously fashioning one for herself, who acknowledged Christ as the central agent of her own salvation and simply followed where he led her. This is a woman who rejected the emperor not just as a suitor, as the Catholic prayers of my childhood recall, but who rejected him as a demigod, as her ruler. This is a woman who preferred Christ's kingdom and did not keep quiet about it. Yet we are so quiet about her now.

So often the Catholic Church lets the brutalizers win the battle on how to speak of women like Catherine, even when the brutalizers are the women themselves. Their wounds are their credibility: "virgin and martyr," as with Catherine of Alexandria; "penitent," as with Kateri Tekakwitha; "stigmatic," as with the Italian Caterinas in their convents. The heroism that brings them to their death hills is often lost to history, but it is often simply left out.

I need better prayers, longer ones. I need their stories to be told in full, and I wish to God that the women who went before me had the privilege of hearing those stories. I think of Caterina da Siena, who was named for Catherine of Alexandria, and prayed to her as patron, as virgin and martyr. I think of Caterina, who near the end of her life, wrote to a nun sick from the mortifications she undertook, entreating her not to let the lesser good of penance get in the way of the greater good of the service of God. Like many anorexics, Caterina felt it right to exercise control over her body by punishing it, and like many religious women, she characterized that struggle with her body as transcendence rather than self-harm. But by the time she was dying from her mortifications, she talked of them as sickness, not sacrifice. She understood, and she warned her sister, that it is laudable and holy to bear crosses, but it is cruel and disordered to make them.

When I went looking for heroes as a girl, it felt like I was presented with a list of categories rather than a book of names: the virgin-martyr, the mollified dissident, the foundress in the field, the mystic in the cloister. Too often I was handed tropes, not women, as jewels in the Church's crown. And all the while, I was so often treated as a trope, not a woman, in the Church: an over-imaginative little girl, a feminist menace, a crazy teenager, an easy target. I work to give my patronesses context because I need it for myself. I need what they had, a fuller story, hidden in Christ.

My confessor was willing to envision that in me, the way he envisioned it in his daughter, whom he named for her vocation to holiness. That generosity of vision helped me start from the beginning, to remember that I am more than my painful history, that I am destined for glory and that I already have the means to pursue it—starting with my name. It was a remarkable thing to impress upon a young person. I imagine he got the idea from the gospel.

👛 👛 👛

In the end, I am Catholic because I always have been. I don't find that passive or sad or strange, and I don't find it to be unfair to my journey, either. A few weeks after I moved back to my hometown after college, a family friend died. The Catholic parish I grew up in was set in motion, as we always are. We organized meals, said Masses, got coffee more often, thought to check in more. We prayed together. We are healing together. I fell back into this rhythm without really noticing it, analyzing it, understanding it, because grace is often something you see in the rearview mirror.

That is what I told the priest at my childhood parish when I went to make my confession and profession of faith to be received back into the Catholic Church. This is a way of life that makes sense to me, one that was inscribed in me a long time ago. It is the one Catherine of Alexandria gave her life hoping to establish, the one Caterina da Siena spent her life trying to preserve. It is their context, and it is mine.

I am Catholic because of women like Katarina av Vadstena, the daughter of the great saint Birgitta, who became a widow like her mother, who became an abbess like her mother, who befriended Caterina da Siena while on business in Rome, who died in peace in her home country of Sweden, of whom we know hardly anything personal. We know nothing of her personality, her spirituality. Instead, she is a footnote in other women's stories. Of all the women my name gave me, she is the one dearest to my heart, because she is the sign of the past I know to be rightfully mine and the future I want to make: so full of holy women in their full diversity that some only show up to provide context for others.

I am Catholic because I know the Church is not my trauma, or the half-stories I inherited about my patronesses, or the anxieties I'm still working through. It's just this: messy people living and dying together, among the people and place God gave them.

Each Sunday, I sit in the same pews I sat in as a child, imagining that heavenly posse. I still do, but without the irony, the characterization as distraction. If we take the Church Triumphant seriously, my grade-school imagination is not far from the truth. It is here, in these pews, in this church, that I have begun to see a place open up for me in that vibrant sisterhood. I see the women God gave me, the place God gave me, and the experiences God gave me, and I understand my name as what it was meant to be after all: an entry into the communion of saints.

An Annotated Bibliography

Bell, Rudolph M. *Holy Anorexia*. Chicago: University of Chicago Press, 1987.

> In this study of Italian women mystics, Bell threads medieval asceticism and contemporary anorexia together as gendered pursuits of control. This book taught me to distinguish these women's asceticism from their sanctity, and proposed that the ways in which their self-harm was used to further agendas in the Church do not necessarily map onto actual theological or spiritual mandates. In short, this book was a relief, in a way that only an outsider's tranquil argumentation can be.

Bonaparte, Darren. "A Lily among Thorns: The Mohawk Repatriation of Káteri Tekahkwít:ha." Paper presented at the 30th Conference on New York State History, Plattsburgh, NY, June 5, 2009.

> The story of Saint Kateri's life as I have presented it here is drawn principally from Bonaparte, a Mohawk historian. His work is unique not only for his emphasis on historical and cultural context but his portrayal of Kateri as one among many young Native Christian women involved with intense ascetic practices.

Hügel, Friedrich von. *The Mystical Element of Religion as Studied in Saint Catherine of Genoa and Her Friends.* London: J. M. Dent, 1908.

> I am undoubtedly a bit hard on von Hügel, who spent seven years writing a book on Caterina da Genova and displays a profound respect for her mystical contributions. If he uses the word "virile" a little too often and uncomfortably insists on the word "thirst" to describe her desire for God, he can hardly be faulted for a lack of enthusiasm.

Hughes, Cheryl C. D. *Katharine Drexel: The Riches-to-Rags Story of an American Catholic Saint.* Grand Rapids: Eerdmans, 2014.

> Hughes dove into the archives of the Sisters of the Blessed Sacrament to bring Saint Katharine to life. The saint's letters especially shed light on her practical character and humble spirituality.

Hugo, Victor. *Les Misérables.* Translated by Charles E. Wilbour. New York: Knopf, 1998.

> In book one, chapter three, the bishop of Digne draws particular attention by preaching the protection of "those upon whom society falls most heavily," namely women and the poor. "As we can see, he had a strange and peculiar way of judging things," the narrator remarks. "I suspect that he acquired it from the Gospel" (21). I nod to Digne in reference to my confessor in order to emphasize just how radical his compassion felt to me. Decency always does, I think.

Jamison, Leslie. "Grand Unified Theory of Female Pain." *Virginia Quarterly Review* 90 (2014) 114–28.

My observation on women saints' wounds as their credibility is cribbed from a dinner discussion of this essay
hosted by Leah Libresco Sargeant. Unfortunately, I can't
remember which participant came up with that phras-
ing, so I'll credit Jamison entirely. In this piece, she
admonishes those who would let fear of romanticizing
female pain stop them from engaging truthfully with it. I
thought of that lesson often while writing my own essay.

The Life and Doctrine of Saint Catherine of Genoa. Translated by Cornelia
Augusta Peacock Connelly. New York: Christian Press Association
Publishing Co., 1907. [Transcribed by Kathy Sewell. Grand Rapids:
Christian Classics Ethereal Library, 2000.]

Libresco, Leah. "When People Offer Me Their Weaknesses as Strengths."
Patheos: Unequally Yoked, June 18, 2015. http://www.patheos.com/blogs/
unequallyyoked/2015/06/when-people-offer-me-their-weaknesses-as-
strengths.html.

> In this blog post, Leah reflects on a discussion she hosted
> about the Benedict Option, a proposal for the renewal
> of Christian community first developed by Rod Dreher.
> She had asked participants to share possible resources
> for this group of Washington, DC–area Christians—for
> instance, a flexible work schedule that could accommo-
> date babysitting. At some point, people began to name
> emotional resources: you can talk to me about depres-
> sion, or recovery. I was at that discussion, and it affected
> me as profoundly as it did Leah. This conversation gave
> life to the concept of emotional hospitality that I discuss
> in this essay.

Mantel, Hilary. "Holy Disorders." The Guardian, March 4, 2004. https://www.
theguardian.com/society/2004/mar/04/mentalhealth.health.

> I first learned about Rudolph Bell's work on "holy an-
> orexia" in this piece, in which Mantel emphasizes the
> isolating, rebellious nature of anorexia in the ascetic tra-
> dition. "Most nuns fasted to keep the rule: the anorexics
> fasted to break it," she writes. "Most nuns fasted to con-
> form to their community: the starvation artists aimed to
> be extraordinary, exemplary."

Sarkeesian, Anita. "Tropes vs. Women in Video Games." *YouTube*, uploaded by FeministFrequency, 2013–present.

> My lament of being handed "tropes, not women" in the Church has its basis in an enormous body of feminist criticism that analyzes stereotypes of women in many contexts. That said, Sarkeesian's media criticism first called my attention to the ways in which reducing women to stock characters removes their agency, and their humanity.

Scudder, Vida Dutton, trans. and ed. *Saint Catherine of Siena as Seen in Her Letters.* London: J. M. Dent, 1911.

> In this essay, I reflect on two of Caterina da Siena's letters, published here as "To Sister Daniella of Orvieto clothed with the habit of Saint Dominic who not being able to carry out her great penances had fallen into deep affliction" and "To a religious man in Florence who was shocked at her ascetic practices."

Via Angorosa

Gabriel Blanchard

I come into the chapel.
The pavement is worn smooth by the cares of years,
Smooth and sad and kindly underfoot.
Quiet, I walk from pew to pew,
Searching for a lonely place to kneel.
The altar is alight with flowers:
Sphered amaranth, mallow, and asphodel,
Bellflower, willow's branch, and eglantine,
Rue, morning glory, and blue columbine.
Stone, white, angelic faces guard the gates
As the priest extends his arms, facing away from me.

The epistle side is full of people
Praying pointedly beneath pointed windows,
Chaplets flashing like so many pearl necklaces
With crosses hanging lightly at the ends,
Their hands washed clean in holy water.
I ask "Is this seat taken?" and the mass of them
Turn terrible faces toward me, shouting "HUSH."

The gospel side is full of people

Chatting with each other, in tee-shirts and tube-tops

And tan lines where their habits used to be,

That have been stripped from them

By self-absolving, magisterial hands.

I ask "Is this seat taken?" and the mass of them

Turn hungrily and seize me, screaming "ALL ARE WELCOME."

I stumble, and fall in the nave,

Abrading my knees on stone;

The bruises bloom like purple irises.

Rise and walk.

Another pew, another, another.

Here I see one I know, and stop there, crying, "Simon!

May I sit here?"

The family man looks up from his Hours,

With edifying illuminations on the sins of the flesh.

He lisps, "I'd rather not; my children are here with me—

You understand. Please don't make noise.

Everyone else is being quiet;

Mass is about to start."

He thrusts me firmly forward

So that I slip again upon the pavement,

Shocking my knees and the heel of my hand.

Another pew, another, another.

And there, a purple-cardiganed, grey matron. "Veronica,

May I sit here?"

She looks up from her demagogic missal

And flexes scarlet nails with golden rings.

"You sit right here; we'll fix you up,"

Takes a fistful of condoms from her purse

And proffers them, each stamped with Mary's face,

Her skull split in a leer of boundless love.

My back aches with the weight of walking

And the sweat comes on my face like blood.

Further forward.

"Our Lady of Law, pray for us!" shouts one.

"Saint Matthew Shepard, pray for us!" screams another.

"Our Lady of Normalcy, pray for us!"

"Saint Mary Daly, pray for us!"

"Our Lady of Anathema, pray for us!" the versicle.

"Holy Zeitgeist, have mercy upon us!" the responsory.

Their loves rub my ears raw;

Divine things are always veiled in mystery.

Every seat is full. I am standing at the rail, between
  the transepts, under a void.

My brow burns,

My chest hurts,

My feet and hands are stinging.

The windows loom above me, out of reach.

I strike my breast and make my invocation:

"I am sorry if I offend you all, because I dread

The pain of heaven and the loss of hell,

Although you are all good, washed white,

And I am bloody, bold, irresolute.

Weep not for me, daughters of Jerusalem, weep not for me;

Weep for your pious children who process behind me!

Our fathers' hearts are turned from us, provoking us to wrath,

And we, God's bastard children; our inheritance

Rejection letters from a host of houses,

An empty cradle where a clan dead-ends,

A white rose withered and a ring of fool's gold,

And this chapel where we Christians love one another."

I seize my scapular, rip off the cross,

And cast it from me;

Why should I bear it?

A third time I fall, striking knees hands chin face upon the floor

At a crack in the stone

And blood seeps from my head.

I lie before the rail and wait to die.

Step, step, step.

The chancel gate is opened;

The priest in a pillar of incense stoops down to lift me up

And bears me into the sanctuary,

Cradling me at his breast. He rests me on the cold altar stone.

I have seen his face before:

Lean, simple, worn by the dry eastern sun,

So full of laughter that the altar feels soft.

I understand nothing.

A darkness descends upon my eyes,

And as I fade into the unknown cloud,

It comes to me:

There is no place that I would rather die.

I hear his voice, faint and far above.

"I break you as bread, I crush you as the grape,

And I shall make of you a mystery

That your darkness may illuminate your father's
    wandering sons . . . "

And then I heard no more.

Notes

ll. 7–9, *Sphered amaranth . . . blue columbine*: Each of these flowers has a traditional symbolic meaning. Amaranth represents perpetual love; asphodel, eglantine, and rue stand for anguish and regret; mallow and morning glory represent being consumed by unrequited love; bellflowers symbolize loss; and willow and columbine signify betrayal and desertion.

l. 12, *The epistle side*: As one enters a normal Catholic church building, the epistle side is on the right, and the gospel side is on the left. (Due to alterations in the liturgy since 1965, this distinction is less prominent than it once was.) The associations of right and left, in our current political climate, hardly require elucidation.

l. 16, *Their hands washed clean in holy water*: Cf. Matt 27:24.

ll. 26–7, *I stumble . . . on stone*: Cf. the Third Station of the Cross, Jesus falling under the weight of the cross.

l. 28, *purple irises*: Purple is a penitential color, commemorating the robe in which Christ was clothed by the Roman soldiers in mockery before His death. Irises, because of their sword-like leaves, are sometimes used as a symbol of Mary as Mother of Sorrows.

l. 31, *Here I . . . crying, "Simon!"*: Cf. the Fifth Station of the Cross, where St. Simon of Cyrene is ordered to help Christ carry His cross (as in Matt 27:32). Cf. also the passage early in T. S. Eliot's *The Waste Land*, in Part I, "The Burial of the Dead," ll. 69–72.

ll. 40–1, *I slip . . . my hand*: Cf. the Seventh Station of the Cross, where Jesus falls a second time.

l. 43, *Veronica*: The traditional name of the woman represented in the Sixth Station of the Cross, who wiped the face of Jesus as He walked, thus creating a unique relic. (The name is sometimes thought to be a corruption of the Latin *vera icon*, "true image," but it may be a Latinization of the Greek name *Berenike*.)

l. 46, *scarlet nails with golden rings*: Cf. Rev 17:4.

l. 52, *the sweat . . . like blood*: Cf. Luke 22:44.

ll. 54–59, *"Our Lady . . . the responsory*: A litany is a form of prayer consisting in a versicle, said by one person, and a responsory said by all. Most responsories in litanies to the saints are "Pray for us," and in litanies to God, "Have mercy on us." *Matthew Shepard* was the victim of a homophobic assault, and his murder spurred immense discussion on the value of hate-crime legislation; *Mary Daly* was a professor at a Jesuit college, famous for her heretical views (particularly on sexual topics) and for barring male students from certain of her classes; *zeitgeist* is a word derived from German meaning "spirit of the age."

l. 62, *transepts*: It is traditional in Latin Catholic parishes to lay out the church in the form of a cross, with the altar at its "head" and the congregants seated in the "body." The two "arms" are called transepts, and often contain small side chapels. The central area is frequently surmounted by a tower or dome, especially in larger churches.

ll. 67–9, *I strike . . . of hell*: Beating the breast is perhaps the most ancient symbol of penitence in the Catholic tradition. One of the conventional acts of contrition, designed for use in the sacrament of penance, begins with the lines, *O my God, I am heartily sorry for having offended Thee, because I dread the loss of heaven and the pain of hell.*

l. 71, *bloody, bold, irresolute*: Cf. the witches' prophecy from *Macbeth* IV.1: *Be bloody, bold, and resolute. Laugh to scorn / The power of man, for none of woman born / Shall harm Macbeth.*

l. 72–3, *Weep not . . . behind me!*: Cf. the Eighth Station of the Cross, where Jesus speaks to the women of Jerusalem, itself derived from Luke 23:27–31.

l. 74, *Our fathers' . . . to wrath*: Cf. Mal 4:6 and Eph 6:4.

l. 78, *A white rose withered*: Roses are rich in symbolism, standing among other things for romantic love; the white rose is also a traditional symbol of secrecy.

l. 79, *this chapel . . . one another*: "See how these Christians love one another" was, originally, a sort of proverb used by Roman pagans to comment on the extent of Christian generosity. Its repurposing as a sarcastic remark is, in all likelihood, nearly as ancient.

ll. 80–1, *I seize . . . from me*: A scapular is a devotional object resembling a necklace, worn around the neck (usually under the clothing), and typically associated with promised graces. Some, notably the Brown Scapular of Our Lady of Mount Carmel, which is probably the most popular, are normally produced with a miniature cross or crucifix attached to the strings. Some scapulars require the wearer to wear them continuously, as an act of faith, to be eligible for their benefits (the Brown Scapular included).

l. 83, *A third time I fall*: Cf. the Ninth Station of the Cross.

ll. 88–9, *The chancel . . . of incense*: The chancel or sanctuary is the part of a church building containing the altar, where only the clergy and their assistants normally go. Though it is rarer today, churches were often built with a low wall or fence separating the chancel from the nave (the main body of the church, containing pews), generally with a gate in the middle. For the pillar of incense, cf. Exod 13:21–22, 30:1–8. For the whole movement, cf. Revelation 4.1.

l. 97, *the unknown cloud*: Cf. the Middle English mystical work *The Cloude of Unknowynge*, whose author urges the adept to forsake every kind of image of God and meditate solely on His being.

l. 101, *"I break . . . the grape*: Cf. 1 Cor 10:16–17.

Made in the USA
Monee, IL
19 August 2022

11973054R00080